stories
from an open
country

essays on the
yellowstone river valley

edited by william l. lang

foreword by michael p. malone

Western Heritage Press
Billings, Montana

Distributed by the University of Washington Press
Seattle and London

The Western Heritage Center is a museum reflecting and interpreting Yellowstone River Valley life. Accredited by the American Association of Museums, the Center is free to the public with funding provided by Yellowstone County, memberships, donations and grants from a variety of public and private foundations. As an educational program of the Center, the Western Heritage Press publishes material relating to the Yellowstone region. Proceeds from the Western Heritage Press benefit the Western Heritage Center.

Stories from an Open Country: Essays on the Yellowstone River Valley is part of a comprehensive project, "Our Place in the West: Places, Pasts and Images of the Yellowstone Valley from 1880-1940," funded by the National Endowment for the Humanities. "Our Place in the West" consists of a long-term exhibit, public programs called Gatherings, which were presented throughout the Yellowstone Valley, and publications including *Stories from an Open Country*. Oral history excerpts included in this publication were funded by the Montana Cultural Trust.

First edition limited to 2000 copies

© 1995 Western Heritage Center, Billings, Montana 59101

ISBN 0-9628215-1-9

Design: Heins Creative, Inc., Billings, Montana

Printing: Color World Printers, Bozeman, Montana

Cover Photograph: *Wild Horse Herd*, Evelyn J. Cameron, Photographer, Western Heritage Center

Library of Congress Cataloging-in-Publication Data
Stories from an open country: essays on the Yellowstone River Valley/ edited by William L. Lang.
     p.   cm.
  Includes index.
    1. Yellowstone River Valley–History. I. Lang, William L.
F737.Y4S76 1995
978.6'3–dc20   95-43313
                                               CIP

preface

Elk River is the Crow name for the Yellowstone. To French fur traders, it was *La Roche Jaune*. "Open country" was the term William Clark used to describe the Yellowstone River Valley in his journal documenting the Lewis and Clark expedition. Bill Tallbull, a Northern Cheyenne spiritual leader, tells of his people's perception of the Yellowstone as "a river with sacred places by its banks." Lillian Stephenson, who came to the Yellowstone Valley as a young girl in the early part of this century, witnessed a landscape far different from the fertile, tame Midwest. She described the area as formidable. It was "a big country . . . there were no fences." August Sobatka had a similar experience: "I thought I'd come to the jumpin' off place." In countless interviews with people of the Yellowstone, the landscape is described as "open land," "great country," "real hard country," a place where "many hearts were broken."

The "open" Yellowstone country ranges from soaring granite mountain peaks and alpine meadows to rolling prairies, cutbanks, and rimrocks dramatically edging the arable river bottom. It is a landscape weathered by time, shaped and sculpted by a variety of cultures. Rock cairns, tipi rings, petroglyphs, and pictographs mark the trails, campsites, and spiritual places of the early Plains Indian cultures. Ruts carved by wagon trains, tenuous fence lines, bridges spanning the river and creeks, solitary homesteads, and grain elevators marking the railroad lines symbolize the American dream of progress and westward expansion in the Yellowstone Valley.

While promotional material painted an image of abundant opportunities in the Yellowstone Valley—fields of wheat, barley, pastoral farms—photographers voiced their experiences and stories through images recording everyday life in the Yellowstone River region. Images of ranches, steamboats, small towns, brandings, picnics, school children, irrigation ditches, parades, and industry reaffirmed a need to describe, to document, to come to terms with living in this "open country."

As large as the states of Vermont, New Hampshire, Connecticut, and Massachusetts combined, the Yellowstone region challenges the imagination. The texture of the land, the expanse of the horizon, and the mythic Yellowstone River form the foundation or the "jumpin' off place" for *Stories from an Open Country.* With names such as Clark's Fork Bottom, Hell Roaring, Wibaux, Sweetgrass County, Muddy Creek, Emigrant Peak, Medicine Rocks, and Absaroka, the Yellowstone landscape serves as a stage and setting for interpretations exploring one place in the American West.

Stories from an Open Country: Essays on the Yellowstone River Valley was developed as part of a comprehensive project "Our Place in the West: Places, Pasts and Images of the Yellowstone River Region from 1880 to 1940." Planned and implemented by the Western Heritage Center and funded by the National Endowment for the Humanities, "Our Place in the West" consists of a long-term exhibit, a series of public programs called "Gatherings," which were presented in communities throughout the Yellowstone Valley, and publications including *Stories from an Open Country.*

In addition to funding from the National Endowment for the Humanities, the Montana Cultural Trust provided funding for an oral history component to "Our Place in the West." The oral history project, "The Real West: Portraits of Farming and Ranching Families in the Yellowstone Region," explored the traditional cultures of farming and ranching in the Yellowstone River Valley, thus providing real life stories and experiences which have been integrated into the exhibit, audio-visual programs and publications.

Stories from an Open Country combines the work of several historians and writers who have been studying the Yellowstone Valley, Montana and the western United States. The book includes photographs taken by professional photographers documenting United States Bureau of Reclamation projects to many snapshot photographs found in family "shoe box" collections. Recollections and life stories of many individuals representing the region's diverse ethnic and cultural heritage—Plains Indians, Mexican-Americans, German-Russians, Scandinavians, western Europeans, Slavic and eastern Europeans, Irishmen, Scotsmen, Welshmen, as well as "immigrants" from the Midwest—link the essays and provide another layer of interpretation.

As with the exhibit and public programs, *Stories from an Open Country* brings together historians and scholars and the voices and visions of men and women who shaped and formed this region. From the project's inception, "Our Place in the West" encouraged and fostered interaction and dialogue among scholars and people in the Yellowstone Valley. Many of the authors whose work is featured in this book participated in the planning of "Our Place in the West" and presented programs for the "Gatherings." A community resource committee and volunteers provided the spark and breadth to all the components of "Our Place in the West."

Special thanks go to the program staff at the National Endowment for the Humanities, particularly to Timothy Meagher in the Museum Division of Public Programs for his belief in "Our Place in the West." All the project consultants, including Carroll Van West, Robin Winks, Barbara Allen Bogart, Laurie Mercier, Joe Medicine Crow, John Peters-Campbell, George Horse Capture, Brad Larson, Mary Clearman Blew, Signe Hanson, and Kathleen Tandy invested their talent and enthusiasm over and over again.

Staff at the Western Heritage Center, including Amy Roach, Mary O'Keefe, Elaine McClurg, and Al Gehring, continually energized the project. Their dedication has been commendable. Community Historian Rom Bushnell traveled hundreds of miles in the Yellowstone Valley interviewing individuals and researching archives. Rom also organized and introduced speakers at "Gatherings" presented at the MonDak Heritage Center in Sidney, the Custer County Art Center in Miles City, Little Big Horn College in Crow Agency, Dull Knife Memorial College in Lame Deer, and the Livingston Depot Center in Livingston, Montana.

The publication team included Emily Witcher, a summer intern at the Center, and Jim Heins, a graphic artist who designed all the publications for "Our Place in the West." This publication would not have been possible without the help of two remarkable volunteers—Charlotte Gage for her work with the archival material and Martha Fregger for her work transcribing many of the oral histories featured in *Stories from an Open Country*.

Others who assisted with this publication included staff at the Montana Historical Society, the National Archives, the Library of Congress, and the Minnesota Historical Society. For the oral history component of this project, thirty-two individuals shared their time, family photographs, and many meals with Community Historian Rom Bushnell. Pat Soden, marketing director at the University of Washington Press, arranged for the distribution of *Stories from an Open Country* to an audience beyond the Yellowstone Valley.

Two people deserve special recognition for their contributions. Despite all the pressures and responsibilities as the president of Montana State University, Michael Malone graciously wrote the introduction for this book. While serving as the long-distance editor of *Stories from an Open Country*, Bill Lang divided his time between teaching at Portland State University and his work as director of the Center for Columbia River History in Vancouver, Washington. With Bill's expertise, the book took shape and the interviews from the oral history project became the bridges linking the essays and writings.

Stories from an Open Country is not meant to be a conclusive history of the Yellowstone Valley. Rather, this collection of writings, photographs, and personal experiences creates other "jumpin' off places"–other trailheads venturing toward our quest to understand the American West. For as Wallace Stegner eloquently summarized in a personal letter referring to this project and our intent: "There is no better way to find out who we are, than to study the place we find ourselves in."

Lynda Bourque Moss
Director
Western Heritage Center

foreword

The Yellowstone Basin embraces an enormous swath of the American West, a swath so large and so diverse in terrains and subregions that it seems, in some respects, to be a microcosm of the West itself. Regionalists might argue indefinitely whether the Yellowstone Country is more unique or more representative than another place: it depends entirely upon what one chooses to emphasize.

Like most of the West's great river basins, the Yellowstone heads in the high mountains, descends through timbered and increasingly dry country, and emerges into lower arid lands. But the Yellowstone presents these variations in particularly extreme contrasts. It heads, after all, in the most spectacular and famous headwaters region in America–Yellowstone National Park–amidst grand lakes, canyons and waterfalls. The river flows north through the lovely Paradise Valley, then bends northeasterly on its long course, through narrow meadows and valleys bracketed by timbered ridges and magnificent mountain clusters to north and south. On the lower half of its long, 670-mile odyssey to its juncture with the Missouri River, just across the North Dakota state line, the Yellowstone drains a remarkably broad and dry expanse of the northern Great Plains.

In its configuration and current state of development, there are several key facts to note about the Yellowstone Basin. For one thing, as the river flows to the northeast, its drainage system is very limited from the north. The divide to the north lies quite near, so that the larger portion of central Montana drains northward into the Missouri, via sluggish tributaries like the Judith, the Musselshell, and the Redwater. The major portion of the basin lies, instead, to the south, with large tributaries like the Big Horn, Tongue, and Powder with headwaters deep in Wyoming. And then there is the rather remarkable fact that the Yellowstone is the only major river in the West to remain undammed on its mainstem, although large tributaries such as the Big Horn and Tongue are dammed. In fact, the flow of the Yellowstone, as it crosses the North Dakota state line, is actually larger than that of the more diverted Missouri.

Like so much of the dry, interior West, the Yellowstone Basin is energy country. The deep-lying oil deposits of the Williston Basin, centered in the North Dakota city of that name, reach well into the Yellowstone Valley east of the Dakota line; and even after 45 years of pumping, these wells are economically important to communities such as Glendive and Sidney. The newer and shallower Belle Creek Field near Broadus is also a continuing major producer. Of course, the basin's true energy bonanza lies in the enormous, shallow-lying coal seams that are located primarily in the drainages of the Rosebud, Tongue, and Powder rivers that rise to the south of the Yellowstone. These low-sulfur, low-BTU coal deposits constitute one of the world's greatest fossil fuel resources. Currently, they are mined both to load unit-trains bound for power plants in the Midwest and Northwest and to generate electricity directly at the cluster of Montana Power's coal-fired thermal units at Colstrip. Relatively low prices and tough competition have kept coal mining at modest levels, but the reappearance of energy crises like those in the 1970s could quickly change all of that.

Another distinguishing feature of the Yellowstone Country is its paucity of human population, which is far from unusual among western regions but is nonetheless striking. Even though approximately 30 percent of Montanans live in the basin, along with a fair proportion of Wyoming folk, the valley has only one urban area, few towns of any size, and a very scattered rural populace. Nearly all of the basin's population centers are located along the river itself, from Livingston in the upper southwest to Sidney in the lower northeast. Of these, Billings and the surrounding irrigated bottomlands (which in frontier times were called the "Clark's Fork Bottom"), with a metro population of roughly 120,000, is the urban hub not only of the Yellowstone Basin but also of a broader region that includes the Upper Missouri drainage to the west and north. Otherwise, only two small cities along the river approach 10,000 in population—Livingston and Miles City—and only two others hover around 5,000—Glendive and Sidney.

The prime reason for the lack of population is the simple fact that the remote Yellowstone Basin, like the northern plains-intermountain region generally, lacks industry and almost any other "value-added" sources of employment. It is energy country, but it is especially agricultural country, and generally marginal agricultural country at that. Truly intensive agriculture is practiced only on the choice irrigated bottomlands of the big river and some of its tributaries, lands that grow not only grains but also hay crops, sugar beets, corn, and safflower. Montana's only two remaining beet-sugar refineries are in the valley, Great Western at Billings and Holly Sugar at

Sidney. Some of the Yellowstone's benchlands can produce dryland wheat, but most are suited only for grazing, and here—as throughout Montana generally—the greatest resource is rangeland.

However limited the basin is in population or industries, it is certainly rich in tradition and in the aura of "the West." In fact, few regions of the West could match the Yellowstone Country for its embodiment of the frontier mystique. It is, of course, Indian country. The Crows, who once occupied even the mountainous country of the Yellowstone's upper reaches and the lovely rangelands of the Judith Basin, are now situated on a reservation that sprawls across the Big Horn drainage and is rich in coal resources. The much smaller Northern Cheyenne tribe inhabits a reservation to the east that is also rich in coal reserves.

As the essays in this volume nicely attest, the Yellowstone Basin exemplifies the nearly full panoply of the frontier experience. While the mining rushes had only a limited impact on the upper valley, the other waves of the nineteenth- and early twentieth-century frontier movements—fur trading, transportation, livestock, Indian wars, homesteading, entrepreneurs—crested fully here. Some of the West's most spectacular Indian-white encounters occurred here, not only the Little Big Horn battle, but also the Rosebud, Fetterman, Hayfield and Wagon Box encounters, and others. More importantly, the entire range of human experience happened here, as can be seen in all of the following essays, particularly those by Bill Tallbull and Mary Clearman Blew. Even Hispanic immigrants found a typical western range of experiences in this northern region, as Laurie Mercier's essay reveals.

While the interesting essays in this volume do not and cannot offer the reader a comprehensive history of the Yellowstone Basin, they do provide a fascinating and enlightening insight into the range of human experiences there and how they have affected the place. From its high mountain plateau lakes and waterfalls to the broad vistas of its eastern plains, the Yellowstone Country is an epic slice of western America, whose broad horizons and fascinating history find ample elaboration in the following pages.

Michael P. Malone
Montana State University
Bozeman

in the yellowstone: river, myth, and environment

william l. lang

In the Yellowstone's West, our stories are about living close up with natural things, about what we have done to our place, and about what has happened to us. Like other stories told in the American West, many of these are full of talk about challenge, struggle, and achievement, sometimes breathing an expansiveness and boastfulness that is ultimately self-congratulatory and other times expressing relief at survival. The storylines usually include overcoming obstacles, dominating a place, and gleaning natural resources from a land that is reluctant to give them up. Their plots are about people who succeed because they persist and live right. We recognize them as environmental as well as mythic tales, because they reinforce the belief that the West is powerful and exceptional, that things happen differently here.

American exceptionalism is a mainstay of our literature, especially in stories about the West. In Yellowstone Country, those stories are rife with the idea that the region made character, that people stayed here or came here because of its physical and spiritual power. Native oral traditions focus on the unique combination of animal spirits, landscape, and people. The Crow people, as Chief Arapooish told a fur trader in the 1830s, knew that: "The Crow country is a good country. The Great Spirit has put it exactly in the right place." No place, Arapooish proclaimed, could be better for human beings. Two generations later, whites who coveted the same lands echoed Arapooish's pronouncements. An 1882 promotion for settlement called the region Edenic, with a "salubrity not surpassed anywhere in the United States."[1]

The specialness of any place is arguable, but it is undeniable that relationships between places and people are a kind of protean glue that contributes to our understanding of human history. Those relationships are the heart of our most powerful stories, where the perception of the geography, the connections people have made with the land, and the mythic images that adhere to place compose a natural and cultural biography. People make these places. They invent descriptions and invest themselves in their region, engaging in a correspondence between themselves and the landscape they inhabit. In that process, which is as mysterious as it is variable, the mixture of description and myth create distinctive portraits of place that are dynamic and changeable. They are creations of the human mind, "a way of seeing," as geographer Denis Cosgrove has explained, but they begin with the land itself.[2]

The Yellowstone Country is dominated by open spaces, sage plains, and mountain-ribbed uplands, where aridity is the dominant pattern of life. Water matters here. It is a place where, as Arapooish described it, "the air is sweet and cool, the grass fresh, and the bright streams come tumbling out of the snowbanks." Where that water ran, who was able to use it, and how it was used often made a difference in who succeeded and who failed. The water runs in cut-bank streams and rapid-strewn rivers, dropping from the high country through narrow canyons to a broad alluvial valley. In the center of that valley flows the Yellowstone River, the life chord of this expansive region of open but fractured landforms. The region's history is in large measure the river's possession, a creation of its influence. Place is, as Yi-fu

Tuan has explained, "an archive of fond memories and splendid achievements" that is housed in its physical realities. To understand the human history of a place requires knowing its environmental history. To understand the Yellowstone Country means understanding the Yellowstone River and what it has meant to the people who have lived with it, used it, and coveted its wealth.[3]

The Yellowstone River begins its 671-mile length as a small, north-flowing channel formed by tributary creeks on Two Ocean Plateau south of Yellowstone National Park. The main feeder to Yellowstone Lake, the Yellowstone runs out of the lake—the largest high-altitude lake in North America—cutting its way through rhyolite and basaltic canyons that extend north through Yellowstone National Park to the Paradise Valley and then flowing east and northeast through a broad corridor to the Missouri River near the North Dakota-Montana state line. The river's 70,102 square-mile drainage basin includes major north-flowing tributaries—the Clark's Fork, Bighorn, Tongue, and Powder rivers—twenty counties in two states, and more than three million acres of land. In its upper reaches, the river is a plunging, canyon-scouring torrent, falling more than half of its 5,800-foot drop in the first 100 miles of its course. But in its lengthy valley sections, where it falls just over one-third of its total descent, the river is a braided stream with sandbars, islands, and channels.[4]

The river's conformation is the product of massive geological, volcanic, and glacial forces. Yellowstone Lake—an expansive 1,350-square mile caldera—was created during North America's most explosive volcanic eruption. A stupendous volcanic upheaval thrust 500 million-year-old rocks from sea floor to 10,000 feet above sea level, creating the plateau that gives rise to the river. A series of glaciations ground and moved rock from the plateau northeastward in carved valleys that carried ice sheets and their glacial burdens out onto the Yellowstone Valley floor in alluvial deposits that make up much of the river's landscape.[5]

The Yellowstone is a river known in three parts by both its native inhabitants and non-Indian invaders. The first section, most of it within present-day Yellowstone National Park, is high-altitude and canyon-cutting, a swift and bold river. The second section runs cold and clear through an upland valley, from Livingston to the Bighorn River, with some rapids and numerous channels, and still cold and clear. The third section flows in prairie country, enlarged by the silt-carrying Bighorn, Tongue, and Powder rivers that make it roil brown. Crow, Cheyenne, Blackfeet, Lakota, and other Indian tribes hunted and lived along the river's lower and middle sections, only infrequently visiting the Yellowstone Plateau, where game was relatively scarce and snow blocked easy passage much of the year. White explorers first described the Yellowstone in 1805, when Francois Larocque investigated the region for furs, and the following year, when William Clark descended the river on the Lewis and Clark Expedition's homeward route. Clark drew the first map to show the river's course and wrote the first descriptions of its environment.

On the Yellowstone near the mouth of the Clark's Fork, Clark described the river as "rapid and much divided by islands." Downstream near the famous landmark he named "Pompey's Pillar," he characterized the river as "reagulilarly Swift much divided by Stoney islands and bars also handsome Islands Covered with Cotton wood." Back from the water course, Clark seemed to revel in the "extensive Country around, and the emence herds of Buffalow, Elk and wolves in which it abounded." The Yellowstone's image was rich in resources for the hunt, a vast wilderness that seemed to preclude agriculture. The expedition's leaders recommended building a fur trade fort at the mouth of the Yellowstone and another at the mouth of the Clark's Fork, where "there is sufficiency of timber to support an establishment, an advantage that no position possesses from thence to the Rocky Mountains." In short, the Yellowstone was a country inviting the extraction of natural resource wealth.[6]

In the wake of early explorations of the Yellowstone, most whites invaded the region with one thing on their minds: gleaning the area's wealth. Their understanding of the Yellowstone's environment boiled down to where and how they could acquire marketable resources, first in animal furs and later in precious metals. When they could, these pursuers of gain employed Indians or made them temporary allies in their game. That was true especially during the era of the fur trade, when success depended on gathering animal pelts, not in controlling land or access to land. Arrangements between American Fur Company men and Indians, for example, enabled that company to dominate in the competition among trading companies to strip the Yellowstone region of beaver, marten, wolf, fox, buffalo, and other valued skins. For the Indians, these tenuous partnerships brought wealth, a sometimes much needed protection against enemies, and a measure of control over their destiny.[7]

The environmental image of the region as a natural resource cornucopia grew large as the exploits of Jim Bridger, Hugh Glass, Tom Fitzpatrick, and other mountain men told of a wild country, where adventure melded naturally with extractive industry. It was a romantic image that veiled real environmental consequences. The fur trade devastated animal populations along the Yellowstone and its tributaries, decimated the great bison herds, and traumatized Indian culture through the introduction of new pathogenic diseases. But the greatest environmental consequence may well have been the enlargement of the cornucopian image, which beckoned to the adventuresome and attracted more extractors of natural resources. If the easily skimmed fur and hide resources had been magnetic in their effect on the gleaners, the power of gold and silver deposits was nearly gravitational. Yet, even more to the point of environmental image and consequence, this new pursuit made the land itself an object, with the control and use of water an essential corollary. Indians were of no help here. In fact, they obstructed and stood between the pick-and-shovel men and their desires. Mining demanded control over place, including claimed plots of land, legal rights to water, and local laws to secure ownership in environmental wealth.[8]

Prospectors first surveyed the Yellowstone during the early 1860s, when the strikes on the Salmon and Clearwater rivers west of the Continental Divide were drawing great attention. The finds in the Paradise Valley on tributaries to the Yellowstone brought a rush of sorts in 1863 and even the promise of a town on the river, where miners could dig up the streambed and sieve out placer gold. But the lure of other, larger finds at Last Chance and Confederate gulches on the upper Missouri siphoned off the miners and, soon after, the would-be town builders. Still, they trenched and scoured Emigrant Gulch, staked out claims, and moved tons of gravel. The promise of gilded water had brought them there, and that image drew others, even as the mining enterprise failed. By 1866 Frederick and Phillip Bottler had established a homestead ranch near the river, and N.P. Langford and others had begun work on a major road down the Yellowstone to link newly platted Bozeman in the Gallatin Valley with Fort Laramie on the Oregon Trail. By 1870, a dozen prospecting parties had found color in scattered defiles in the Absaroka Mountains, a crude wagon road had been punched east into the upper Yellowstone from the Gallatin Valley, and two adventuresome expeditions had made the hydrothermal wonders of the Yellowstone Plateau known to the world.[9]

This activity signaled the introduction of new and environmentally disruptive forces in the region. Ditches had been dug, streams diverted, and roads cut. Ironically, the mining had taken place in the more remote Yellowstone regions, far from the locus of the fur trade in the Bighorn region and farther downriver at Fort Union. Before the gold-seekers invaded the Yellowstone Valley, the government's interest had focused on the river as a travel route and its potential for settlement. In 1859, Capt. W. F. Raynolds led a military exploration of the lower river region. He considered the upper Yellowstone country "terra incognita," an inaccessible region of wonders, if Jim Bridger's tales of boiling springs, geysers, and burning rivers were true. Raynolds explored the river course as a potential travel corridor, believing that emigrants would pour through it, just as they had two decades earlier on the Oregon Trail.[10]

Raynolds's characterization of the lower Yellowstone region as an area dominated by an "absence of trees" and few pastures, however, portrayed it as inhospitable for agriculturalists. In the Powder River valley, for example, he found "water of poor quality." On the Tongue River, where he located water that was "clear and cold," there was little or no grass. Although Raynolds recorded seeing buffalo on the plains in numbers that "defy computation," he noted that wildlife abounded only in the low, riverine areas. The Yellowstone Raynolds described was not the region portrayed by fur traders and gold-seekers. It was a place of forbidding terrain and aridity, save along the water courses. His report made clear that access to water would provide the key to any development of the area.[11]

By the mid-1870s, the environmental reputation of the Yellowstone Country included images of a wilderness once teeming with fur-bearing animals, a magical place of roiling waters, a potential El Dorado, and a river that could accommodate steamboats. For non-Indian settlement, the most important image was the river as causeway. Another government-sponsored exploration of the river—under the command of Lt. Col. James W. Forsyth—brought the steamboat *Josephine* to the mouth of the Clark's Fork, just short of 500 miles from the river's mouth. The advent of steamboat service helped spur the citing of river towns—including Coulson at the mouth of the Clark's Fork—that vied to supply the newly created army posts and potential emigrants. By the late 1870s, a few adventuresome settlers had used the Homestead and Desert Land acts to stake out claims to the bottomlands near the Clark's Fork and to build up an infant community. More than three hundred individuals paid taxes in 1879 to the recently created Custer County.[12]

The river had drawn these settlers, especially once the steamboats offered easier transportation, but it was water used as a resource that would hold the greatest promise for the area's agricultural future. Early promotional literature drove straight at the point by describing the Clark's Fork Bottom area as the gateway to a 16-million-acre agricultural bonanza. All the region lacked was government promotion in land sales and irrigation projects. Impetus for new investment came between 1883, when the Northern Pacific built its mainline up the Yellowstone, and 1891, when Crow Indian Reservation lands were thrown open for white settlement. By 1905, the population ballooned from a few hundred in 1882 to more than 12,000.[13] The generative force in the boom was water applied to the fertile plain. "Irrigation," civil engineer Walter Graves wrote in 1894,

> has not only rendered it possible to live in the so-called desert, but it
> has made it so profitable and delightful to live there that this same
> desert has become a veritable Mecca for Utopian seekers.[14]

From the Yellowstone's first irrigation project, the "Big Ditch" that the railroad's land company developed during the 1880s, to the building of the High Line Ditch in 1899 and the creation of the Huntley Irrigation Project under the Newlands Act of 1902, the secret to creating an agricultural empire was in spreading river water on the benchlands above and away from the river course. Irrigation, as one commentator wrote in 1908, was the "magic wand" that had transformed a desert

> into fruitful fields and verdant meadows. . .its face
> is adorned with numberless hamlets, and the deep yellow
> of a golden harvest—the home of a million of free men.

This hyperbolic image reached for a future that surely would have seemed beyond possibility to Raynolds, Bridger, and Langford, but it had helped create a new landscape that brought wealth. By the early twentieth century, this new Yellowstone promised to be even more dynamic and utopian, if the engineers—the river's new alchemists—could have their way.[15]

There is an inherent power in irrigated landscapes that has held sway in human development for more than three millennia. The ability to command water has long made and maintained empires, but the twentieth-century American version, as Donald Worster explained, created an especially ambitious and even gluttonous variant. The new hydraulics used advanced engineering to escalate the domination of nature to high levels. With Promethean intent and capitalistic purpose, the engineers sought means to impound and direct the use of water to make over the Yellowstone in service of an agricultural empire. The irrigated Yellowstone had been a compelling vision from the time of the Big Ditch, but during the 1920s the river's water became commodified and transformed as a source of wealth unto itself.[16]

The great promise of reclamation in the arid West had dissipated by the early 1920s, the result of too many crop failures on some reclamation projects and not enough water on others. But it was also true that the dryland farming strategies had resulted in another kind of disaster, when drought ravaged the high plains between 1917 and 1920. In the Yellowstone Valley, where water was abundant in its rivers, irrigation remained the best hope for the empire builders. Government engineers followed their earlier assessments of the Yellowstone River, formed in surveys conducted on the lower river in 1909 and 1910. Glendive, Billings, and other communities along the river had requested improvements to aid navigation, but the engineers had determined that the costs were too high. Irrigation was a better use of the Yellowstone's waters than channelizing the river to make it friendlier to barge traffic. At Intake—eighteen miles below Glendive—a network of canals carried water to an arid landscape. By the mid-1920s, the agricultural production of sugar beets would justify the building of a sugar reduction plant at Billings. The focus was on water for "beneficial use," which meant applying technology to free running water to capture it, channel it, and direct it to wealth-creating projects.[17]

Because the damming of the river downstream of the main tributaries would be ineffective in flood control and provide less control over the delivery of irrigation water, the engineers looked upstream, above Livingston. They proposed schemes to dam the river at Allenspur Gap, a narrow cut through a limestone ridge; at Yankee Jim Canyon, a black-rocked slice in the

Absaroka Mountains, or at Yellowstone Lake. The Allenspur proposal (first suggested in 1902) dreamed of a 250-foot-high dam that would back water upstream for more than fifteen miles and create a reservoir with 1.5 million acre-feet of water. The engineers had nixed building dams at Allenspur and farther up the river at Yankee Jim Canyon because of costs or, in the case of Yankee Jim, because the impoundment would have put the town of Gardiner and the entrance to Yellowstone National Park under several feet of water. The Yellowstone Irrigation Association proposed a six-foot-high dam at Yellowstone Lake that would store nearly half a million acre-feet of extra water in the lake. The glorious water jewel of Yellowstone National Park would become the source for irrigation projects throughout the valley. The irrigators had created a wholly new view of the Yellowstone River, with a reservoir at its inception and a regulated flow running downstream through the national park and the valley beyond. By damming Yellowstone Lake, the engineers hoped to avoid conflicts with other interests on the river.[18]

Montanans liked the idea. Senator Thomas J. Walsh introduced legislation in the Senate, and the Montana legislature petitioned Congress to let the engineers have their way with the river. But the engineers, Walsh, and Montanans met a buzz-saw opposition among defenders of Yellowstone National Park, including the influential eastern conservationist, George Bird Grinnell. Grinnell called the irrigationists "spellbinders" who conducted "night schools of oratory" to convince the unthinking that a new, cornucopian day would dawn on the Yellowstone if they could impound the river's water.[19]

The defenders of the national park, especially those from outside the region, killed the Yellowstone Valley Irrigation Association's plan, but the dream of an irrigated empire on the Yellowstone lived for another day. The dam at Yellowstone Lake had contrasted two images of the river, one epitomized by the breathtaking falls and great river canyons in Yellowstone National Park, the other characterized by the Huntley Project and the dam at Intake. They were the product of two distinctive creations, one vested in the natural resource bounties of the region, which included the national park, wildlife, and scenic beauty, the other entangled in modern engineering and the siren of economic development, which included the building of a hydraulic empire in the Yellowstone bioregion. By 1932, the second vision had refocused as the irrigationists directed their attention at the entire

Yellowstone River Basin and convinced Congress to divide control of the river's waters between Wyoming and Montana. The extended drought during the 1930s brought pleadings from existing irrigation district managers for more water, which could come only with new projects. After nearly three years of negotiation, representatives of Montana and Wyoming agreed on the Yellowstone Compact, which carved up the bioregion to "provide for the equitable division and apportionment of the use of the waters of the Yellowstone River," a grand plan to "conserve and use the waters of the river so as to obtain maximum benefits." The compact's new vision was explicitly instrumentalist. It put the water in Yellowstone National Park off limits but opened up the rest to the impounders' schemes. The river had been transformed into a new political landscape.[20]

In the American West, mixtures of water and politics nearly always become volatile. The thirsty lust for what the saturated have, and between them they often create a fractious and litigious landscape. In Montana, the access to water followed the doctrine of prior appropriation, which meant that the owners of the oldest water rights stood first in line to fill their buckets. In the Yellowstone, that spelled trouble for the hydraulic dreamers who wanted unlimited water without hamstringing restrictions. As originally drafted in 1935, the Yellowstone Compact tried to apportion all water resources, for to do less would leave too many restrictions on agricultural and industrial applications. But the compact writers failed to get the state legislatures to agree. The sticking point was all of those prior allocations, water rights that were held by entrenched interests. The plan stalled on this issue until 1950, when the compact commissioners agreed to allocate only non-appropriated water resources.[21]

The irrigators began dreaming an altered vision, one that would create their future from the Yellowstone's unallocated water. That new vision focused on the Yellowstone mainstem, and also on the Bighorn, Powder, and Tongue rivers, where major storage projects might supply both the holders of both old water rights *and* new projects. Wyoming and North Dakota got assurances that they would retain their historic access to water, while the irrigators pursued plans to spread more water in Montana. By the early 1960s, the engineers were back on the Yellowstone mainstem at the Allenspur dam site, proposing a 380-foot-high dam to block the Yellowstone and create a 33-mile-long, 4.2 million acre-foot reservoir in the Paradise

Valley. The Allenspur project drew fire from sports fishing groups and local residents, forcing the Bureau to shelve the proposal. Meanwhile, the dam-builders had concluded controversial negotiations with the Crow nation to construct a massive dam on the Bighorn River, discussions that divided the Crow people on the issue and included opposition from respected leader Robert Yellowtail, the dam's namesake.[22]

Completed in 1968, Yellowtail Dam transformed the Yellowstone River bioregion. By blocking the river's largest tributary and creating a 41-mile-long reservoir, the dam so regulated the outflow from the Bighorn Reservoir that the Bighorn River lost more than a quarter of its area through the destruction of islands, gravel bars, and limitations of river flow. More important to the watershed, the dam demonstrated the potential for huge water storage projects. Spring runoff turned the Yellowstone and its tributaries into torrents that irrigators and other potential water users saw as "wasted" flow, water that could be put to "beneficial use" through impoundments and application to the land. As long as the focus remained on flood control and irrigation, however, reservoir projects would be limited by the feasibility of agricultural development in the basin, which depended on availability of capital, government willingness to support reclamation projects, and world commodity prices. Nonetheless, the Yellowtail Dam had shown the way to a new Yellowstone future.[23]

What could not have been predicted was the potential shape and dimension of that future. Rather than agricultural it would be industrial, and on a massive scale. Yellowstone Country residents first heard about industry's plan to radically change their landscape in 1971 with the publication of the North Central Power Study, which projected the construction of more than forty coal-fired electrical power plants on the Northern Plains, twenty-one of them in Montana using Yellowstone water. The reason was coal—millions upon millions of tons of strippable mineral wealth just below the surface in the Yellowstone Basin. With efficiency and economic gain as their guiding principles, planners reasoned that stripping and burning the coal in mine-mouth electrical generating plants would maximize the use of the resource and their return on investment. A furor of opposition and political activity followed disclosure of the plan, including the organization of citizens' groups, volatile public debates, and state legislation.[24]

The prospect of an industrial landscape in the Yellowstone challenged historic expectations, which assumed that stock raising and agricultural development would always dominate. Even though the irrigationists had introduced new hydraulic technologies to the Yellowstone, the portent of siting smokestacks on the lands where Custer fell, where the XIT wranglers rode, and where the Crows and Cheyennes hunted threatened the meaning of the place. More environmentally threatening, however, was the steam plants' thirst for Yellowstone water, which revived the Allenspur dam idea and other diversion and reservoir projects. The further prospect of siphoning off some of Wyoming's share of the Yellowstone for coal slurry pipelines from the Northern Plains to the Midwest added to the concern.[25]

The coal issue dominated political discussion in Montana during the 1970s, but only a portion of the debate focused on water. Concerns about disturbance of the land, the effectiveness of mine reclamation, and air quality all contributed to the discussion. In the state legislature, increased support for environmental protection aided the anti-coal development forces. The result was sweeping laws to protect air and water quality, including a 1973 statute that forced all water rights holders to refile or lose their rights. The following year the legislature enacted a three-year moratorium on all major allocations of Yellowstone Basin water. By the mid-1970s, even with additional pressures brought by the Arab Oil Embargo, Montanans said "no" or "go very slow" to coal development and especially the use of Yellowstone water.[26]

Citizens throughout the Yellowstone Basin, perhaps worried by the covetous glare that outside interests had directed at their water resources, generally supported protection of water quality; some advocated permanent moratoriums on building steam plants or strip-mining coal. The Yellowstone's environmental health became a competitor with development, and the preservation of water quality led the state to warn that rivers in the Yellowstone Basin might "be severely affected through dewatering from water demands . . . from potential coal development in this region." Using the measurement of dissolved oxygen in the water as an index of health, especially for fish, biologists urged the state to draw a hard line on "beneficial use" of Yellowstone waters. The focus on riverine protection combined with an increase in eco-tourism and a boom in flyfishing and other recreational use of the Yellowstone stimulated a revolutionary change in Montana's water laws. In pathbreaking legislation in 1978, the state approved instream reservations of water as a "beneficial use." The state could now keep water in the river for fish and other aquatic life.[27]

The crisis atmosphere created by the North Central Power Study and the intense statewide discussion about the future of the Yellowstone Basin had created another, new image of the Yellowstone—a river of the highest quality for fish culture and the last major free-flowing river in the United States. A generalized movement composed of ranchers, environmentalists, recreationists, and tourism promoters forced the public to ask hard questions about the Yellowstone and its fate. Journalists came to report on the controversies and to marvel at the river and its environment. Increasingly, the Yellowstone took on an aura of a river inviolate, a wilderness place where tourists could experience the quintessential West that had been lost to development in so many other places. The spell cast by the Yellowstone was nearly magical, evoking paeans from the newly initiated. "Its voice created an ache inside of me," one newcomer to the river wrote in the 1980s, "that only going [downriver] could satisfy."[28]

The late twentieth-century image of the Yellowstone fully embraces western exceptionalism. Even though employment in natural resource industries has declined by half since 1970, there is more agricultural, municipal, and industrial development lining the Yellowstone's banks than at any time in its history. Nonetheless, it is advertised as the last of the "untamed" rivers, a river of mythic quality, a piece of history. It is the "wild" Yellowstone and its romantic aura that promise to fuel the next surge of economic development on the river. Most economists predict that the river's future is likely to be an environmental one, where tourism, recreation, and the health of the river will significantly underwrite broader economic development. A 1994 survey of residential subdivisions along the upper Yellowstone confirms this direction; only one-third of the riverfront between Pray and Livingston remains free of subdivisions.[29] In ways that make the river appear to circle back on itself, the Yellowstone has become an icon of its own history. And in ways both palpable and abstract, the river has become a melding of its romantic pasts and its utilitarian futures. The Yellowstone's exceptionalism, if it is real, rests in the texts of the stories told about how people have used the river, schemed it, and continue to revere it as the unifier of a vast and open country.

"The meat supply is gone, you know. Matter of fact that was the government's idea of getting rid of their food supply. Then we've got 'em. So they decided, encouraged the buffalo hunters to go kill them all which they did in that quick and grand fashion. . . . Well some tribes further east, like the Sioux, Cheyennes, Arapahos, others, suffered quickly without buffalo, because they didn't have anything else. But we were fortunate here in this area where the Crows live that there was still a lot of animals to eat. Elk, lot of elk. That's why they call this river, Elk River, just loaded with elk. And of course, antelope, a lot of antelope. I see a bunch everytime I leave Hardin to come to Billings. . . . Then, of course, sometimes they eat prairie chickens. Lot of prairie chickens here, sage hens. But we shied away from fish. They didn't like fish, Crows. Lot of fish north of, in these streams, creeks, a lot of good trout but they don't take time to sit down and fish. That's kind of a dull way of getting food. . . . And then we have a lot of roots here. Wild carrots, wild turnips. Used to be all over this country. So the Crows did not suffer as suddenly and as dramatically as the other tribes when the buffalo, the main supply of meat was gone."
Joe Medicine Crow

"Loss of land. That was in 1904 when we lost, well let's say lost the ceded strip area. But now the legal people say it's not ceded in the classic sense, you know. Ceded is giving it all, letting it go. But now we got the mineral rights. Quite a bit of the land up there was never allotted

to anybody so they kept allotting small tracts. . . . So they started allotting hundred and sixty acre tracts up there in the so-called ceded area to young people, now it is all gone, except tribal blocks up there that are still there. . . . So that's still going on and now in 1904 around there we had about 3,000,000 acres left in our reservation proper after giving about 2,000,000 to the government. So of that 3,000,000 acres, half of that's gone now. Just slightly above 51 percent that we still own in trust. But the rest is owned by non-Indians, and fee patent status, private land." Joe Medicine Crow

"Little Big Horn College has a Crow language department. We have experts who have studied linguistics in universities, and so forth. They've developed a Crow grammar book with alphabet and all that sentence structures and all the old grammar and dictionaries, so we're trying to keep it that way, too. We are losing it at home, but we are trying to keep it going in our schools. At one time the federal government came to the Crow reservation and financed bilingual classes in all the public schools there. And the little kids, five, six, seven year grade kids started studying the Crow language. Whoa, pick it up quickly. Even non-Indian students pick it up. Pretty soon they're reciting ABCs in Crow, singing lullabies, and beginning to speak the Crow language . . . . The Crows have what we call, what I would call cultural persistence." Joe Medicine Crow

2

a cheyenne story

as told by bill tallbull
to george horse capture

We are the *Dzitsistas* and have a long and proud history. *Dzitsistas* is our own name for ourselves and means "The People," but we are more commonly known as the Northern Cheyenne Indian people and live on our reservation located on the south central portion of the Yellowstone Valley. The history of our People beqins with the creation.

The Creation Story begins with the story of a person who was floating on the water. He didn't have a name because he was the *only* person. With him were sea birds of various sizes who would fly high in the air looking for a place to nest or to walk around on, but they couldn't find any because the entire world was covered with water. It was the wish of the person to find a piece of soil, so he asked the birds to help him. From time to time they would dive downwards, but they were not successful: they couldn't reach the bottom. This went on for a long time until one day a little mud duck thought that if everbody else tried and failed, maybe he should try too, so he dove down and finally he came back up with some mud in his bill. The person thanked the mud duck and carefully made a little ball of the mud: he kept rolling it until it became dry. As it turned into powder, he said, "I am going to blow this upon the water and land is going to appear." So he took this powdered soil and began to blow it upon the water. When the soil hit the water, land started to appear, moving the water aside. Land kept forming. The tired sea birds left the water to walk upon the land.

Later, the Creator, who caused all of these things to happen, feeling something was missing, formed a man and a woman, and he blew life into them. Then he began making things so that these two people had something healthy to eat: he created plant and animal life. At that time the Creator had put a spirit into everything he made. He put the spirit in the earth, and into all plant life, and man and woman. The man and the woman soon developed a physical and spiritual relationship between themselves and with the other things around them. When they approached plants, the plants would say, "We have been waiting for you. We are here with you. Take what you need of us. You are our relatives." And wherever they went the animals would say the same thing.

One day, the woman said to the man, "Let us talk about a few things. First, how are we going to cut this meat, how are we going to prepare this food?" The man said, "Give me two stones." He then hit the two stones together until a knife fell out. "Here is how we are going to cut the meat," he said. The women said, "Now, we can make tools and spear points out of the stone, but there are other important things we have to talk about. You are a man and I am a woman. You have the power of the sun and I have the power of the moon. There are certain times in the moon phase that I will shed blood. This is going to be the beginning of reproduction so that babies will always come from us. They then began to determine what would be needed to survive. The crow and the magpie came to him and and said, "We will give you some feathers to decorate your spear. We are the two birds that find meat first, and we eat quickly before the others arrive. We will give you the power to do so too." So he took the feathers of the crow and magpie and decorated his spear.

At that beginning of time, the animals were huge and the people had to hide in caves to defend themselves. One of the animals was the huge bison who was a flesh eater, and they could not fight him properly with just spears. Once the bow and arrow appeared the bison said to themselves, "Run, there is a powerful person here, he is killing us. Take what you got in your mouth and run." So the buffalo ran, taking what flesh he had in his mouth. Today there is a piece of fat next to his windpipe, and to us it is human fat, and when we kill a buffalo that is the one part we throw away and do not eat. Some people call this flesh sweetbread.

When the people had the bow and arrow, they could defend themselves a lot better, and became successful as bowhunters. They began to venture out from that place to search for food. When the animals were scarce they would have to migrate elsewhere to find water, plant life, and animal life to avoid famine. As they wandered one time, they came to an ocean and began to follow the shore: at that time they were fish eaters. Following the seaboard the people still had to run from the huge animals and would hide under the giant tortoise shells, when necessary.

The spiritual part of life was created at that time, and the people strived to maintain a spiritual harmony with everything. This was during the ice ages. At certain times spirits would come to them and the people would give them a gift, so a friendly relationship developed between them and the sun, the moon, and the stars. These spirits were called upon by the people in times of famine and the spirits would take pity upon them and restore the animal herds, plant life, and rain. At that time they were still migrating from place to place and were somewhere up north around the Great Lakes country. When they were in Ontario, the glaciers came again after disappearing for awhile and covered the country, forcing the people, the animals, the plant life, into caves. They remained there until the ice receded again. One day a man saw sunlight outside, and then the people moved out into the world. That is the ancient history of the Cheyenne.

Another part of our history tells of a time when we came to a marsh area in southern Canada and the people could not cross. They devised a raft and a boat out of reeds, and some of them attempted to cross the marsh and in order not to get lost in the reeds they would take branches and stick them in this marsh as markers. They finally made it across and began to migrate south: the animals and the people were all heading that way. They came to the upper reaches of the Mississippi River and started to venture out into the prairie. There they met an animal that drove them back. This animal has a name, a Cheyenne name. It was described as a fierce bovine animal who had horns, a mane like a horse, short hair like a horse and was a flesh eater. Like the horse, it had teeth on both jaws, so they called him the double teeth buffalo. One could hunt them by their smell. They were very fierce animals. When the people saw him on the prairie, they would start running and would climb trees for protection. When they did this the animal would do strange things: it would play dead, sometimes for days. When the people got down off the tree, the animal would get up and kill them. It would always get the hunters, the ancient hunters, until one time for reasons unknown they began to disappear and the people could continue their movement. According to hisory's research, such an animal did exist in Minnesota 9,000 years ago.

A long time ago there was a special man who came into camp. He was a holy man and had been sent from a mountain far away. He had predictions for the people. He said that there was going to be a people that were coming from the east, and they were going to come and keep coming. There will be no ending of them. They will cover this country: those people were the white people. The prediction also warned that the new people will even ask for your flesh.

He said that the next thing that was to happen to the people was the coming of the horse. "Once this animal comes, your life again will change. You will no longer touch the ground when you cross this country. You will go from one mountain range to another in a single day." And he said there is going to be another animal that will come to take the place of the buffalo because the buffalo was going to disappear. "This new animal will be spotted and have a long tail." When it takes the place of the buffalo he cautioned them not to eat of its flesh, because when you butcher this animal his muscles will still jerk even after it is dead. (Cows do that.) He said, "If you eat of that flesh, then you will be a nervous people. Your children will not do well on cow's milk because this animal is alien to this country, and will eventually poison itself."

So these were some of our predictions that were given long before any white man came to this country and one day they began to happen. The white American did come here as well as the horse and even the cow, and they began taking our children from our homes to send to boarding schools and into Headstart and Daycare. He said, "When those children return to you they are not going to know anything anymore about their Indian life."

These are some of the origin stories told to me by my family, relatives, friends, and our elders. These events are all true and they, with many things, form an important part of our Cheyenne history. As important as the origin stories are in our world, our history continues to this very day with each generation and tribal member expected to somehow contribute to it.

As an elder now, I can look back on my life and determine if I have done my cultural duty. It is a real concern to us to pass on as many tribal traditions as possible.

My early home was located on an isolated part of the reservation at a place called Muddy Creek, about twelve miles from Lame Deer. We had a little log cabin on my mother's allotment, three miles down the creek from my grandparents' place. When my mother was about to give birth to me, my uncle came down from their place on horseback to be on hand. It was a cold winter evening in January 1921. When he rode down, the moon was out but it was cloudy at the same time. Soon he began to hear wolves howling, especially one. He knew it was a mother wolf calling for her pups. She kept howling for one whose name was Featherwolf. "Where are you, Featherwolf?" she howled. It seemed strange to him for all of a sudden he could understand the language of the wolves. When he finally got to the house to see my mother, I had just been born, so he just stood by the stove and took off his gloves. My mother said, "It is a boy." After awhile he said, "I have a name for him." She waited for him to say what that name was, but he didn't say it until later. He recounted to my mother the ride he had made and that he heard a name from the wolves. He said, "I want to give him that name, Featherwolf." At that time he was close to those animals, and my mother understood, in her heart, their importance to him, so Featherwolf is my Indian name. As I grew up and began to understand some things, my mother told me about what my uncle had said and I wanted to learn more. Being an inquisitive youngster, I kept asking her, "When is he going to see me? When is he coming over?" My mother replied, "Just be patient, the day will come." I was talking about the animals.

Later, I had moved away from the homestead and purchased a piece of property south of Busby, and one winter night coyotes came to my door! I ran them off. The next night the same thing happened. The third night the same. I thought, "This is getting strange." All of a sudden I remembered that night forty years past. The wolves are no longer here, but their cousins, the coyotes remembered. When the coyotes came back the fourth night I went out and made an offering to them. I said, "Thank you for coming. But always leave a good word. If you have words to give me, let them be good words. I know you can deceive people, but don't deceive me. I have waited a long time for this to happen." I stayed out there just talking to them. The next night they came again, and I went out and fed them. Several times that year I would go up in the hills on the lunch hour and sit. A coyote would always come and start barking at me. It was good to know such things still happen, although man and animals speak different languages today.

The coyotes continued to talk to me even when I would be away from the reservation, going to school somewhere. I remember walking down the street in Tucson, Arizona, and I heard the coyotes again. I ran to the dormitory and called home to find out what was going on. Nothing happened then, but the next day, I got a telephone call from Ashland telling me that a trailer house caught fire and someone died in the fire. These were the types of information they told me. The warnings gave me an opportunity to pray and ask if something bad was going to happen. There is no way we can stop it, but don't let it happen to my people. It is the only thing I could do. After four years the coyotes quit coming. I don't know if someone shot them, or what happened, but they are coming back again. I've noticed two times now that they have come back. I was in Santa Fe once and had driven up in the hills to a home of a friend. As soon as I opened the car door, there was a coyote. I don't know if they are coming back. These are things I don't know. You just let it happen. Whatever is going to happen will happen.

At the time of my birth, some special sensitivity was given to me. For instance, one day at a ceremony, whirlwinds came, and they followed behind me all night long. And today, at home, when I leave the house and go down to the field, whirlwinds come and bump into me. There are two of them, and they are not ghosts as they sometimes are. These whirlwinds never come to the house. They sit down below here near a chokecherry bush. Whenever I cross the field, they run into me. So I always take my cigarette out and say, "All right," and I smoke to them and talk with them. They watch our place, and run back and forth, but never come to the house. Other power things happen to me, but I just let it happen and don't worry about it. I don't question it.

Indians have a spiritual relationship with all things, and that is why we are different from all other peoples. For instance, I was walking up Medicine Wheel Mountain one time with four other people in deep snow. We were all in line about half a mile from the wheel, near a rock wall made when they chopped out the road, when I saw a movement. At first I thought it was an antelope, because it didn't look like a deer when it stopped and turned around. I had a good look and saw it was a wolf, a reddish one! Then it disappeared over the hill. When I got to that spot I saw it had left no tracks. But I thought, this spiritual mountain has all kinds of spirits, and this wolf is one. Every animal has a spirit, and once they die that spirit goes into the hills and lives until conditions are right and then they come back out. All the buffalo that disappeared are in the hills, too, in the mountains, and all the water creatures that have passed on, their spirits are in the water. So when you go out into the hills sometimes the spirits will appear. They may manifest themselves in many different ways, and you just let them be there. You must never doubt or question what you see, because what you see may be the spirits. We all have to believe in something, because belief is the most important part of our lives.

The preservation laws today, and there are lots of them, usually don't work. They are made by people who have no understanding of the spirit life in this country. In order to protect the spiritual integrity of a mountain or a sacred site, the lawmakers must understand spiritual things. They try, and try, but it doesn't work because they separate government and religion. Nobody wants to talk about religion, but God is everywhere. The government laws make you think God is far away, beyond reach or they don't even mention Him at all, but He is right here. That belief is so basic to humanity, but they just don't understand that. You know this belief is so basic, it seems kind of funny when you think about it. They don't want to understand that the earth–land–can have spirits and be sacred and must be saved because of that.

The ancient warrior, or the ancient hunter, a long time ago, was sent out from the village to explore the valley. This ancient person went out and explored. The trees, the plant life, the animal life, the water, he saw it all, but he also found a spirit life in the valley that made the area compatible for people to live in. Spiritual compatibility was what he was looking for. When he went out to the good places he would mark them with rock piles on the hills. They could be seen or feel the spirits and said that this must be good land: this must be a good valley. Follow the valley, follow the rock cairns because they show spiritual compatibility of the site. There are such cairns along the Tongue River, indicating that this is a good valley; the water is good, the animals are good, and the people who live there are good. Together they show the compatibility of the area.

There is a place where there are no cairns for a space of about four miles. On that red shale hill a spirit resides. It is not compatible. He has a face on each side of his head, and has a name. He wears a necklace made out of human ears: they are strung together. When people would stop there he would come down, so people avoided him. When the ancient people mapped this valley with cairns this area was left bare. Further up you see the rock cairns again, so this is how we read this valley. Archeologists have been going back and forth there, but they don't know how to read the valley the way the Indian people do, they don't understand the spiritual nature of the valley.

The Yellowstone River played a role in our history. It marked the northern boundary of our space, and when invaders came here we would chase them that far. One story that shows this is about a medicine man named Ice. He went on a war party. He dreamed that enemy were coming, so he went on a war party against them. He took his party across the Yellowstone River and traveled to the Musselshell River, where a coyote on a hill howled and told him, "Your enemy is a little ways from you, you'd better hurry." Soon after that they were getting ready to get up in the morning and move when a magpie flew up, saying, "Your enemy is right next to that tree over there." They saw the enemy as they saw them, so they took off and crossed the Musselshell to an island where a coyote gave them further advice that allowed them to be victorious. Upon their return, when they crossed the Yellowstone River, they knew they were safe.

People have animal friends that help them. When the enemy would take horses from the Cheyenne they would run long enough to believe they had gotten away. They would stop at the Yellowstone to rest and swim. My people would follow then and retaliate as they relaxed. The Yellowstone River always seemed to be a boundary for the Cheyenne Territory, and we have sacred places by its banks in many places.

I tried to do my best with the most important things in my life—my family and Cheyenne history and culture. Somehow we must pass this knowledge on to two major groups: our children and to the white man. Cheyenne children must know these things because it is a part of them, and some future day they will have to pass it on to their grandchildren. In this way we will always survive. The white man must know of these things too, because they hold a mindless power over us, either actually destroying parts of our tribal heritage or allowing others to do it, usually for votes or for money.

In conclusion let me tell you a little more about us. Each of our elders have a special place where they pray: when they talk to the spirits, they face east. In our country there are trees nearby so they develop a spiritual relationship with the land to the east, with the trees to the east and everything around them. Anyone who cuts down the trees threatens that relationship. The whole village or tribe may use those trees and mountains, they all look to the east. They are part of the people: it is part of their life. Anyone who disturbs that union is disturbing the spiritual welfare of the people. This destruction has happened, and it is very demoralizing.

As a youngster going down to school, there were little trees here and there along the way. Every morning I would say "Hello" and "Good morning" to them, and we became playmates. I played with these trees. They knew who I was and I knew who they were. Whenever I got beat up at school or had other problems, when I passed them on the way home, these

trees would reach out and touch me, saying, "Hey, it is not that bad, buddy."
They made me feel better. These trees were always my buddies. When the
horses were about to trample them, I would run over there and protect them.
A bit away from there is a hill and on it was a big tree. I used to climb it and
sit there and talk to it. I would take some bread and I would give it to the
tree. I developed a relationship with the tree. The tree spirit is a very
powerful spirit and man shouldn't ever destroy them: they are a living part of
the world like us.

As a bit of advice I would like to say we have seen destruction take
place in this country, where plows have destroyed the spiritual harmony of
the earth. They make it difficult for the animals, the birds, to find nesting
places. They have destroyed that harmony that was there for thousands of
years. We have a story that reminds me of what might happen to us. Nearly
sixty years ago a message came to my uncle that said the animals and the
birds were going to leave because of the destruction that was happening to
them. They said that it was too hard for them to continue to live there
because of the destruction of their nesting sites and the destruction of their
food supply. In order to live they would have to move to strange new places.
They decided that they would leave, disappear forever. My cousin looked at
his shocked father and said, "What is troubling you?" But he would not say
anything. For several days he didn't want to eat, he didn't want to sleep, he
just sat there. My cousin rode to several of us and said, "Come on down, let's
go talk to the old man, there is something going on here. I don't know what
it is." So we all gathered together, all eight of us men, and talked to him. We
knew that whatever it was, it must be important and that made us worry for
our families and our way of life. We sat there and talked to him all night, and
all the next day, and half of the next night. Finally he said, "There is a word
that came to me. It came from the Black Hills. The animals and the birds are
going to leave. There are too many bad things happening to their space. I
may tell them not to go but there is no way I make things right for them
anymore. Maybe it is best that they do go, at least they will be safe." We sat
there and the first thing that came to our mind was, "No, don't let them go.
Our lives will be too empty." We asked him, "Could you ask that they stay for
a time? We need animal life and bird life because they are part of us: they are
part of everything that we do. They are part of our life, both physically and

spiritually." So he said, "All right, let me try something. Come back in four days." In four days we drove our wagons back and put up a lodge, prepared all the proper food, and invited him to come in. Everybody was sitting and being quiet. He started a ceremony to talk to the spirit that brought the message. He asked the birds and the animals not to leave even if their life was hard. He asked that they remain with us for a time. He said we need them so that our lives will not be empty. Apparently the animals and birds took pity on us and decided to stay for awhile. If things didn't get better, they may decide to go any time. All of us must do what we can for the animal and birds and the beautiful and spiritual places where they live. What would we do without them?

an undeniable presence: indians and whites in the yellowstone valley, 1880-1940

frederick e. hoxie

Modern communities in the Yellowstone River Valley, like communities in every other part of North America, share one common characteristic: their foundations rest on Indian country. Like people across the continent, the Yellowstone Valley's modern occupants have often turned away from this indigenous heritage. But as they and their counterparts elsewhere have learned, it is impossible to escape the Native American presence. Just as children cherish the feeling that they are the first in the world to walk and talk, Americans have frequently celebrated their own achievements by pretending they are unique and without precedent. But just as children mature by learning to see themselves as citizens of a vast humanity, Montanans in the Yellowstone Valley—like other Americans—have developed a richer view of their own communities by seeing them as part of a grand continuum that runs from the ancient past, through the present, and on into the future.

Several years ago, earth-moving equipment at a construction site near Wilsall, Montana, disturbed two skeletons. Within a short time investigators at the site unearthed more than 100 stone and bone artifacts from the area immediately surrounding these burials. These objects included a flaked, stone projectile point nearly six inches long and worked sections of mammoth bone. Carbon dating indicated that these items were more than 10,000 years old. At about the same time, the construction of the Big Horn Canyon dam near Hardin, Montana, prompted archeologists to investigate historic areas that might be flooded once the river's flow began to back up behind the new structure. These scientists learned that the Big Horn Canyon area contained caves and rock shelters that had been occupied continuously for more than 8,000 years. Their excavations traced a story of human occupation that had begun 10,000 years ago, soon after the retreat of the last glaciers, and continued on into the nineteenth century.[1]

Pictograph Cave, located just a few miles south of Billings, tells a similar story. Beginning in the 1930s, pioneering archeologist William T. Mulloy worked his way through twenty-three feet of debris there, uncovering a virtual road map to the prehistory of North America. His research revealed that hunting peoples had followed herds of mastodon and other large animals into the Yellowstone River Valley as the last ice sheets retreated northward. The hunters developed new techniques and turned to new prey as the environment shifted and they adopted new technologies. Mulloy's data not only confirm the ancient presence of Indian people in eastern Montana, but it also illustrates two important themes in the Native American experience: these original Montanans were both tenacious and adaptable. As reflected in a historical record that stretches across a hundred centuries, their tenacity and adaptability have also been evident in the recent past. In the late nineteenth and early twentieth centuries, as they faced unprecedented levels of disruption and dislocation, the Yellowstone's communities of Crow and Cheyenne people sustained these distinctive traits while struggling to adapt to rapidly shifting conditions.

In 1880, Indians on the Northern Plains looked forward to a period of peace and renewal, after nearly two decades of warfare. The American military appeared willing to retreat to its network of forts, leaving the region's peaceful tribes to exist on their own, and standing ready to protect them from settlers and squatters. Even Sitting Bull, the Sioux leader who had fled to Canada following the Indians' glorious victory over the U.S. Army at the Little Bighorn returned home to Dakota Territory in 1881, apparently ready to give up life as a warrior. In the Yellowstone valley, there were even greater expectations for a tranquil future. The Sioux, who had moved relentlessly westward across the Powder and Tongue rivers during most of the previous century, had been defeated by the U.S. Army and were now confined to a vast reservation that stretched from the Missouri River to the Black Hills. Similarly, the fearsome Blackfeet, who had competed with the Crows for game on the prairies north of the Yellowstone, were now hemmed in by federal troops and split between reserves that straddled the Canadian border. Their neighbors, the Gros Ventres and Assiniboines, people who had often raided southward from their homes along the upper Missouri, were also hobbled and on the defensive. These former adversaries had few resources with which to launch new attacks. The Yellowstone now belonged primarily to the Crows, much as it had a century earlier before the arrival of fur traders and prospectors.

By 1880, bands of Indians speaking a language that whites called "Crow" had occupied the Yellowstone for nearly three hundred years. Expelling the Shoshone hunters who had preceded them there centuries before, and barring others who had struggled to gain entrance to its rich hunting grounds, the Crows had flourished in the shadow of the Big Horn mountains and along the milky river that cut through their land. Over the decades, the group had expanded. Its numbers grew as kinsmen from the Hidatsa villages along the Missouri moved west and joined their ranks. Once gathered in the Yellowstone, the Crows broke into groups of loosely related families and fanned out, stretching north and west to the Judith Basin and south into modern Wyoming. In the process, the Crows became horsemen and traders (they acquired their first mounts from the Shoshones, who had Spanish ponies from Santa Fe). They established productive trade relationships with neighbors and distant relatives to the east—exchanging furs, horses, and meat for tobacco, corn, and (later) guns—while cultivating military alliances with Rocky Mountain tribes and others. By the time William Clark floated down their cloudy river in 1806, the Crows could rightly be called "les beaux hommes," a community of beautiful men and women, rich in earthly possessions and proud of their many achievements.

Seventy-five years after Clark's journey there were only a few Crows who could remember a Yellowstone valley devoid of strangers. Fur traders had arrived even before the American explorers, bringing new technologies and deadly diseases. Smallpox epidemics in the early nineteenth century cut the group's population by as much as 50 percent, and the presence of guns and steel tools inspired changes in both economic activity and social organization. Hunting bands spent increasing amounts of their time processing beaver pelts and then buffalo robes for trade. They acquired a widening array of possessions, from colorful glass beads to canvas and coffee. Wealthy men took multiple wives, and military leaders exerted a powerful influence over tribal affairs. Meanwhile, agreements with U.S. officials in 1825, 1851, and 1868 obligated the Crows to live within circumscribed boundaries and accommodate themselves to non-Indians. Among other concessions, the Crows were forced to accept the idea that the entire language group would live together along the Yellowstone. Meeting at the tribe's agency at Absarokee on the Stillwater River, River Crows who had hunted the upper reaches of the Missouri for centuries and Mountain Crows who had frequently spent an entire year in Wyoming's Big Horn Basin learned that they would not be able to return to their home regions.

Peace in the Yellowstone was relative in 1880. Even though the dramatic conflicts of previous decades were over and the newly erected Fort Custer stood guard over the trails leading east to the Dakotas and north to Canada, a new element had entered the Indians' environment: white settlers. Ironically, the Indians' perception that eastern Montana was now "safe" was shared by non-Indians who actively undermined the peace of the region. Conflicts with newcomers—both on and off the reservation—were a central feature of Crow life in the 1870s and 1880s. As early as 1872, the Crow agent reported that whites were coming onto the reservation by the hundreds,

> killing and driving the game; ... destroying the best of their grazing country by bringing into the country herds of cattle and horses; roaming at will from one end to the other; (and) searching for gold and silver mines.[2]

Conflicts between settlers and small bands of Indians sometimes led to bloodshed. Unfortunately for the Crows and their neighbors, any attack on settlers or their cattle was considered an act of war, while similar attacks by whites were believed by local Montana officials to have been taken in self-defense. The white perception of reservation borders also reflected this dual standard. Most ranchers and settlers who streamed into the valley believed that the reservation boundaries were temporary and should not exclude whites, but tribal members should remain confined and not be allowed to hunt on public lands.

Whites repeatedly accused Indian hunting parties of stealing horses and killing stock belonging to white ranchers whose lands adjoined the reservation. There may have been some cattle killing, for dozens of reports were filed with the Indian Office during the years after 1876, a period when it was also clear that the supply of game in the region was dropping precipitously. Nevertheless, the tribe's agents and the commander at Fort Custer typically testified that the Crows were innocent. In early 1882, for example, Colonel Hatch at Fort Custer wrote that while quarrels with whites were bound to occur, "such frays are unlikely to be espoused by the tribe. The rough element among the whites on this frontier is very hostile to the Indians." Agent Armstrong wrote in the summer of the same year that while Crows occasionally begged for food, they had not done "any great wrong since my arrival at this agency." The following spring, Hugh L. Scott, a young lieutenant who would later become army chief of staff, was dispatched to capture a group of "renegades" who were hunting near the Little Missouri River. Upon his return to his post, Lieutenant Scott reported that "there are no more inoffensive people in the United States of any color than are these Crows."[3]

White Montanans urged the Indian Office to negotiate a reduction in the size of the Crow reservation. In March 1880, the Crow agent called the tribe's leaders together and proposed that they cede to the United States all the lands west of the Clark's Fork of the Yellowstone, territory running from modern Bridger, Montana, to Livingston. The tribe rejected this proposal but the agent was undeterred, selecting a group of six Crow men to travel to Washington to discuss the matter further with the president. Once in the

East and believing that they were hostages, the delegation agreed to the new border—temporarily. Back home, they once again rejected the government's proposal, insisting instead on a new border at Boulder Creek (which flows into the Yellowstone at modern Big Timber). Faced with unanimous opposition, the government relented.

The 1880 land cession (approved by Congress in 1882) kept the government at bay and had a minimal effect on tribal life. The 1.6 million-acre area that the tribe ceded had long since been overrun by prospectors and squatters, and it had never been a place of long-term residence for Crows. More important than the land sale, the negotiations allowed a group of young Crow men to step forward as tribal leaders. Plenty Coups, Pretty Eagle, Medicine Crow, and Spotted Horse were all in their late twenties or early thirties when they spoke out at the 1880 council. They had risen to prominence during the conflicts of the 1870s, but the coming of peace challenged them to develop new tactics and a new agenda. During and after the negotiations, they defended the interests of the Crows living on the reservation without antagonizing their new white neighbors. Their style of politics—defiant but peaceful—would characterize Crow leadership for the next half century.

The men who emerged as leaders in 1880 were increasingly visible during the remainder of the nineteenth century. Spotted Horse, for example, outspokenly opposed the Northern Pacific Railroad's intrusion into Crow country. As the road snaked westward from the Dakotas in the fall of 1880, the young chief met a group of surveyors near Arrow Creek, threatening to destroy their route markers if they proceeded without tribal consent and continued to feed Crow hay to their horses. When the tribe granted a right-of-way through their lands the following year, Spotted Horse spoke up again, waving a knife before the council and threatening anyone who tried to expand upon the terms of the agreement. Even when Crow leaders cooperated, they resented any diminution of their holdings. Medicine Crow tried to explain this position to a group of government officials when he told them why the Crows would not agree to the resettlement of refugee Cheyennes on their reservation. "We want to be friendly with the whites," the young chief declared, but "we don't want the Cheyenne with us."[4]

As Medicine Crow's comment suggested, the tribe was also concerned about protecting its position in relations with other tribes. Raiding continued on a subdued scale throughout most of the 1880s, while visits between reservations opened the possibility of new political alliances with old enemies. In the fall of 1883, the Crows' government agent witnessed one of the most dramatic examples of this new diplomacy. He reported to his superiors in Washington, D.C., that the tribe had "the first friendly visit ... on record" from a delegation of forty-five Oglala Sioux. Led by Red Cloud's old comrade, Young Man Afraid of His Horses, the group appeared in the Stillwater Valley in full regalia and war paint. They stood abreast of one another on the outskirts of the Crow camp, before beginning a dramatic—and clearly well-rehearsed—ritual. With only two leaders remaining in their saddles, the group dismounted in unison and "knelt down with their heads bent forward until they almost touched the ground." Following this ceremony, the delegation was welcomed into the Crow camp. The following spring Two Moon and Roman Nose led similar delegations of Cheyennes to the Little Big Horn. During 1885 and 1886, traditional allies such as the Hidatsas from Fort Berthold also appeared to renew old ties and pledge their friendship. By the summer of 1886, one military officer could report that "the Crows have made peace with all the different bands of Sioux," as well as with their other neighbors.[5]

As the pace of white settlement quickened during the 1880s, tribal leaders grew more vigilant and more sophisticated. They urged the Indian Office to allow them to set terms for land leases to cattlemen and prospectors, and they insisted on having a voice in the administration of reservation affairs. As Spotted Horse declared at one meeting with the tribal agent, "put stock on the reservation, and when we want them off, put them off."[6] Local whites were horrified by such defiance, viewing any sufferance as "coddling" people who did not know their own best interests. Nonetheless, the Crows insisted. They opposed most new railroad construction and saw to it that the government awarded grazing leases primarily to those who befriended and assisted them. Plenty Coups, for example, defended one such agreement with Nelson Story by pointing out that the cattleman had "given my people food for three winters." He also pointed out that Story and other favorites were quick to employ Crows as cowboys and teamsters.[7]

Despite their tenacity, however, the Crows continued to be pressed for further land cessions. Willingness to approve the 1880 sale and the Northern Pacific right-of-way (and a second right-of-way in 1891, that made possible the link between Sheridan, Wyoming, and Billings) bought the Indians time, but the demand for land was insatiable. In 1890, government negotiators pressured the tribe to approve the sale of all their lands west of Pryor Creek. Despite Plenty Coups's defiant cry that "If you white men put in all your money to buy that land you would not pay all it is worth," the tribe gave in to the demands. The Crows extracted a substantial cash payment for the tract, a written assurance that the government would phase out its hated agency boarding school, and a series of other administrative reforms, but the tribe lost control of the beautiful valleys surrounding modern Absarokee, Joliet, Red Lodge, and Laurel.[8]

A decade later, when Indian Office negotiators demanded the sale of all lands south of Lodge Grass and north of present-day Hardin, a united front of tribal leaders initially blocked the proposal. Nonetheless, the negotiators pressed their case. John Edwards, a former Billings merchant who had recently been appointed the tribe's agent, waved an envelope stuffed with $10,000 in small bills before the council, promising to "pay this money" when the agreement was signed. The deal they eventually struck in 1898 severed a final piece of historic Crow country from the reservation, the area between Fort Custer and the Yellowstone. Despite later efforts to reduce their reservation boundaries still further, the dimensions established in 1898 have remained unchanged to this day.[9]

During the twentieth century, Plenty Coups, Medicine Crow, and the other leaders who had risen to prominence during the contentious councils of the 1880s and 1890s became highly skilled at defending tribal resources. In 1908, for example, when Inspector James McLaughlin—the man who had ordered Sitting Bull's fatal arrest in 1890—was dispatched to Crow Agency to arrange for the sale of all "unoccupied" tribal lands, the Crows resisted. Speaking to a gathering of fifty-nine "leading men" of the reservation, the bearded Indian Office veteran struck an aggressive note:

> The increasing white population of this great country demands
> additional lands as homes for settlers. I am telling you the naked truth

when I say that I believe that there will not be a foot of surplus Indian reservation land in the United States that will not be open to settlement in the near future.[10]

The Crow reaction to McLaughlin's proposal was uniform. Plenty Coups spoke first. "I do not want to bargain with the Government or anyone else to dispose of our lands," he declared, "the land is mine and I do not want to sell it at all." Other men rose quickly to echo the man who had been arguing on behalf of the tribe for nearly thirty years. Bell Rock declared, "I do not want any more bargains or sales and I want you to take my words direct to the President." Medicine Crow agreed, as did Big Medicine, the chief of the agency police force. But a series of younger voices were also heard. James Hill, a thirty-three-year-old graduate of the government's Indian boarding school at Carlisle, Pennsylvania, explained to McLaughlin that the tribe did not intend to dispose of any more assets; it wanted instead to develop the property it now controlled. Hill's eyes were on the future. "The reservation that is going to be thrown open," he pointed out, "is one of the principal things that we are going to use. . . . We are going to use every foot of that land . . . and we do not want to sell it at all."[11]

McLaughlin's failed mission precipitated a decade-long struggle to open unused farm land on the Crow reservation to white settlement. The story of that effort, as well as of the Crow resistance to it, carries us beyond the scope of this essay, but it provides an appropriate window through which to view the tenacity and flexibility that continued to characterize tribal life. Not only did the tribe oppose further diminution of their domain, but they did so by drawing on a wide array of new weapons. In 1909, Plenty Coups and other leaders contacted the Washington law firm of Kappler and Merillat and requested that they represent the tribe's interests before Congress and the Indian Office. A year later, acting in part on their attorney's suggestion, the tribe formed a business committee made up of two representatives from each of the reservation's six districts. This group combined the skills of "elders" such as Medicine Crow and Plenty Coups with the education and energy of younger people who had attended government schools and learned the white man's tactics. In addition to James Hill, the younger men included Joe Cooper, George Washington Hogan,

Russell White Bear, and Robert Yellowtail. Determination and these new weapons provided the tribe with effective ways to resist political pressures. Delegations travelled regularly to Washington, D.C., testifying before congressional committees and mobilizing the support of the Indian Rights Association and other reform groups. They also lobbied "friends" who leased their grazing lands to use their influence on the state's congressional delegation.[12]

In the end, the tribe's efforts produced the 1920 Crow Act, a law that allowed for the sale of Indian-owned land but did not provide for the wholesale opening of tribal property to white settlers. The statute divided the reservation among all Crows and allowed individuals to sell their property, placing strict limits on the amount of land to be leased and retaining all subsurface mineral rights for the entire tribe. The Crow Act did not reverse the tide of white settlement or the relative growth of non-Indian economic power in the Big Horn valley, but it contained protections that other tribes in similar situations did not enjoy. It also reflected the sophistication and durability of a tribal leadership that had gradually developed a system for making decisions and sustaining a consensus in a rapidly shifting environment.

Perhaps the most vivid reflection of the tribe's political effectiveness was the speech business committee member Robert Yellowtail made before the Senate Indian Affairs Committee advocating passage of the Crow Act. Referring to President Woodrow Wilson's recent return from the Versailles peace conference and the impending debate over American entry into the League of Nations, Yellowtail observed that the United States had committed itself to the principal of self-determination for all people, "no matter where they live, nor how small or weak they may be, for what their previous conditions of servitude may have been. ... I and the rest of my people sincerely hope and pray," the young man continued, "that [the President] will not forget that within the boundaries of his own Nation are the American Indians, who have no rights whatsoever." Yellowtail compared the Crows to the "small and weak" peoples of the world:

> Mr. Chairman, I hold that the Crow Indian Reservation is a separate, semisovereign nation in itself, not belonging to any State, nor

confined within the boundary lines of any State of the Union, and ...
no Senator or anybody else, so far as that is concerned, has any right
to claim the right to tear us asunder by the continued introduction of
bills here without our consent and simply because of our geographical
proximity to his State or his home, or because his constituents prevail
upon him so to act; neither has he the right to dictate to us what we
shall hold as our final homesteads in this our last stand against the
ever-encroaching hand, nor continue to disturb our peace of mind by
a constant agitation to deprive us of our lands, that were, to begin
with, ours, not his, and not given to us by anybody.[13]

This combination of defiance and legal principle would continue as a central
theme in Crow discussions of the tribe's relationship to the outside world.

During the 1920s, Crow leaders worked to develop the mineral
resources of their reservation and struggled to maximize their profits from
grazing leases on members' lands. They also launched a suit in the United
States Court of Claims to reverse what they viewed as the illegal seizure of
River Crow lands along the upper Missouri in the 1870s (hiring another law
firm to assist them in the process), and mounted a campaign to remove the
reservation superintendent from office. Interest in local politics attracted
large numbers of tribesmen (and women) to meetings of the business
committee, where they debated questions, circulated petitions, and frequently
welcomed individuals who had not been elected to the group to speak. As
one young boarding school graduate declared in 1921, "When the rights of
the Crow tribe are involved, it is worth fighting for. All nations of the
civilized world fight for what they deem their rights."[14]

By the end of the decade, a general council had replaced and
overwhelmed the business committee. Modeled on the general treaty
councils that had brought together groups of band leaders or "chiefs" in the
nineteenth century to meet with government representatives, the general
council became an arena where leaders from different districts competed for
influence and attempted to focus the group on important issues. Charismatic
leaders often captured these meetings. Disputes between their followers
could split the tribe into warring camps, but even at their most competitive
the general council demonstrated an underlying sense of community
purpose. As Barney Old Coyote, an educated young man, proclaimed at one

1925 gathering, "Let us have no faction, create no ill feeling and let us all work for the common cause of our people, the Crow Indians." Today the general council continues to be the Crows' chief decision-making body.[15]

The tribe's tenacious and flexible political leadership succeeded again in the 1930s when Robert Yellowtail, one of the lions the of general council, became superintendent of the reservation, the first tribal member in the nation to oversee government activities on his own reservation. At an elaborate inaugural ceremony in August 1934, Yellowtail announced that "a new era, a new hope and a new deal has dawned for the American Indian." He called for a variety of reforms, including a revision of the cattle leasing process, an Indian preference system in hiring agency employees, and increased development of the tribe's mineral resources. He pursued these goals into the next decade, even though hampered frequently by rivals within the tribe, opponents in the Indian Office, and powerful economic interests in both Hardin and Billings. Nevertheless, he managed to revive economic life, improve the quality of local schools, and raise the spirits of his constituents. When he left office in 1945, there was no doubt that the Crow community would be a permanent part of Montana's future and that Crow political leaders would continue to defend the "rights" of the tribe.

The history of the Northern Cheyennes follows a course that roughly parallels the Crow experience. Occupying a reservation just east of Crow Agency, the Northern Cheyennes first settled in the Yellowstone valley in the aftermath of the plains wars. They had begun the nineteenth century as a single group living in the Dakotas. By mid-century, they had divided into two parts, the northern group allying themselves with the Sioux who pushed west and north in the wake of the last major bison herds, and the southerners moving into Colorado. As the army swept through Wyoming and Montana during the 1870s, the Northern Cheyennes splintered even further into small, refugee bands that spread across the entire arc of the northwestern plains, from the Platte River to the Canadian border, seeking sustenance and sanctuary. During that decade, several groups of Cheyennes began to settle along the Tongue River. In 1884, after the Crows refused to take these refugees (their former enemies) into their own reservation, the government created a reserve for the Cheyennes, establishing its headquarters along the

Tongue River, not far from Fort Keogh (near modern Miles City, Montana). The reservation eventually covered more than 450,000 acres.

During the ensuing decades, Cheyenne leaders successfully prevented local ranchers from gaining access to reservation lands, and, as at Crow, their oppostion formed the beginnings a new generation of tribal leaders. By 1900 their struggle (with support from sympathetic whites) produced a special act of Congress that expanded the size of their reserve through the purchase of land belonging to non-Indian settlers. The Cheyennes' isolated location, together with their ability to muster support from Washington, D.C., earned them a degree of breathing room. In the twentieth century, they developed a tribal grazing operation and managed to prevent non-Indians from purchasing significant portions of their land.

But even as both Crows and Northern Cheyennes solidified their political positions in twentieth-century Montana, making it clear to their white neighbors along the Yellowstone that they would not become "vanishing Americans," other developments within their communities contributed to their sense of achievement and optimism. The two tribes managed to sustain a variety of traditional religious practices. The sun dance, a central element in Cheyenne community life, had been outlawed by federal authorities in the nineteenth century, but tribal members managed to keep it alive by altering objectionable aspects of the rite or by moving it to isolated locations. At Crow Agency, tribal members actually expanded the reach of one central ritual–the tobacco society adoption–and transformed it into a central community event. Even though agency officials condemned those who took part in tobacco society activities, its members persisted, even incorporating one part of their annual round of ceremonies into the reservation's annual celebration of the Fourth of July! Chief Plenty Coups spoke for many other Crows when he assured one frustrated agent that tobacco society rituals did not deserve to be banned. "The old people have only one dance left," he declared, "it is the only dance of our fathers left to us and that is about all the enjoyment the old Indians have. . . ."[16]

Other forms of nineteenth-century tribal life also survived into the modern era. Viewed as innocuous or entertaining by non-Indians, these expressions of traditional Indian culture provided an important focus for feelings of community allegiance and mutual support. Crows and Cheyennes participated in public entertainments in Billings, Sheridan, and other nearby towns, proudly parading in buckskin costumes and setting up their tipis and cottonwood arbors. Both at these performances and at reservation gatherings, tribesmen never passed up the opportunity to punctuate the event with singing and dancing. Music was provided by clubs such as the Crow Night Hawk Singers, and dancing drew costumed people from all age groups into a central arena. Dances ranged from relatively "new" social dances such as the "hot dance" or "grass dance" to older dances such as the Crow Owl Dance.

The preservation of music and dance, viewed by outsiders as an innocent artifact of the past, carried immense cultural significance. Singing groups provided a way for younger people to learn old songs and ceremonies; dancing societies generated a demand for traditional costumes; and the gatherings themselves—enjoyed by whites, but controlled by tribal members—created a forum for distinctly Indian activities. One feature of most dances, for example, was the practice of celebrating a happy event with a "giveaway." People grateful for the birth of a new child or eager to honor an achievement by a family member would accumulate a supply of material goods and simply give them away. As the anthropologist Robert Lowie observed of the Crows in 1910, "what impressed me particularly in the hot dance performance, was the lavish generosity with which members gave away property of all kinds to aged and destitute tribesmen, or to alien visitors. ... I once saw a man strip himself (completely) before a large crowd, giving away all his clothing." Similar celebrations of tribal values occurred during hand games, communal sweat baths, and other purely social and small-scale events.[17]

Culturally, politically, and socially, the Indian people of the Yellowstone valley were an undeniable presence during the first half-century of Montana statehood. Their increasingly articulate political leaders had quickly learned to grasp the levers of power and governmental influence, their religious and social leaders had created forums for the celebration of tribal values and had creatively adapted traditional practices to modern conditions, and their communities had begun to increase. The steady decline of Crow and Cheyenne population during the nineteenth century ended in the first two decades of the new century. By 1940 both groups had begun to regain their former strength. Despite these achievements, however, there was one arena of Indian life that white Montanans could ignore. Brilliantly inventive in politics, religion, art, and social life, the Yellowstone valley's modern Indians could escape neither the reach nor the domination of the modern industrial economy.

In the twentieth century the Northern Cheyennes retained nominal ownership of their lands, but most economic development on their reservation was fueled by outside capital. Cattlemen leased tribal lands, and the tribe's substantial timber and mineral reserves were dependent on external markets. Both coal and timber also required large capital outlays for sawmills and mines—outlays the Cheyennes were unable to make. Without access to the game that had sustained them for centuries, and without the resources to invest in the industrial economy, tribal members had no alternative but to squeeze a minimal existence from their surroundings. Small gardens and family cattle herds supplemented what unskilled labor was available in their isolated surroundings. The government was the principal employer on the reservation and unemployment rates remained high, save during the 1930s when a Civilian Conservation Corps outpost was established on the reservation.

While Crow economic experience in the early twentieth century largely conforms to the dreary fate of the Northern Cheyennes, the Crows began the period with more resources at their disposal. When the town of Crow Agency was founded by the Indian Office in 1884, the tribe's agent believed that, with the buffalo disappearing and white settlers streaming into the Yellowstone Country, the tribe needed to prepare for a new economic order. The Crows largely embraced this goal, as most band leaders agreed to start raising cattle and farming the well-watered bottomlands of the Bighorn and Little Bighorn rivers. The Crows were surprisingly eager to learn new ways of making a living. Having adapted to the plains region centuries earlier and later profiting from acquiring horses and guns and working the fur trade, it seemed reasonable to assume that the community would succeed in this latest effort.

It did not. Despite their shared objective, the tribe and the government pursued separate paths to economic well-being. The Crows believed that making a living would require them to learn new skills and acquire a facility with cash. The non-Indians surrounding them had far more complicated goals. The tribe's agents believed that economic self-sufficiency should be accompanied by a variety of new "civilized" traits: individualism, a willingness to drop old traditions, and a love of daily toil. The group was expected to surrender its collective identity, trading new individual economic relationships for older, tribal ones. The necessity of earning their daily bread, one agent wrote in 1896, would be "an everpresent and a silent but powerful force" for progress.[18]

Differences between Crow goals and the goals of both government officials and white Montanans characterized much of the tribe's economic history. Local government men were eager for Crows to be "productive," but their definition of that term was quite narrow. "There are many shrewd dealers in this tribe," the agent M.P. Wyman reported in 1889, adding that the Crows "realize fully the value of money and demand and obtain a fair equivalent for whatever they may sell." Nevertheless, this former Northern Pacific employee was worried that the Crows' business activity would not be compatible with the interests of their new white neighbors. Wyman wrote darkly, for example, that he had "never seen a tribe more attached to their traditions and older customs than the Crows." Despite their business acumen, it seemed that the community was determined to remain culturally distinct. Wyman added, "beyond a disposition to labor and earn money, which they exhibit to a marked degree, they do not favor progress in our civilization." As community members struggled to farm, raise cattle and maximize their earnings on tribal assets, they were constantly measured by the non-Indians' standards of enterprise. Outsiders rarely examined or understood the Crows' own economic goals.[19]

The Indians' difficulties, however, were explained by more than cultural misunderstandings. When the tribe sold the western portion of its original reservation and moved its agency to the banks of the Little Bighorn, the Crows were the largest population group in the Yellowstone valley. By the turn of the century, the city of Billings alone contained more than twice the number of people as the Crow reservation. Following the sale of tribal lands north of Fort Custer in 1904 and the subsequent creation of the town of Hardin, thousands of white settlers were literally at the Indians' door. More important than population, was the relative wealth of the non-Indian and Crow communities. The arrival of railroads, irrigation, and mechanized farming placed capital-intensive industries alongside modest tribal enterprises. Whites often claimed that the arrival of bustling economic activity in Crow country was a healthy trend that would introduce the tribe to modern methods and bring prosperity to the Yellowstone valley. By 1940, however, that claim had grown thin. The disparity between the economic power of the two communities had grown so large that it had become virtually impossible for members of the tribe to make a living in their homeland.

Adding to that tragedy was the extent to which federal officials (and their local Montana backers) squandered the tribe's assets. Not only was land allowed to pass into white hands through sale and lease, but the cash received by the tribe for these sales was wasted on an extensive system of irrigation ditches in both the Big Horn and Little Bighorn valleys. Between 1884 and 1919, at least $1.9 million was drawn from the tribal account for the construction of irrigation ditches.[20]

The Crows' state-of-the-art irrigation system far outstripped their needs and managerial capacities. When completed, it was intended to irrigate more than 73,000 acres of land and cost in excess of $100,000 per year to operate and maintain. As the project's chief engineer wrote to the Indian Office,

> without proper supervision, no irrigating ditch will remain for any length of time in a serviceable condition. It is no more possible to utilize a self-operating ditch, and secure satisfactory results, than it is a self-operating railroad.[21]

Crow leaders opposed this grand scheme, but their protests were ignored. At a meeting in 1892, Plenty Coups, Spotted Horse, and several others had insisted that they wanted "small ditches" built. Plenty Coups agreed that the project's designers had "a good heart," but he worried that the project would "cost too much money, more money than the Crows want to give up for it."[22] His words were prophetic. No more than 10,000 acres of irrigated land were ever cultivated by tribal members, and the tribe never had the resources to maintain the facility. The bulk of the area under ditch passed into the hands of non-Indian lessors or purchasers. This process was accelerated during the years of rising grain prices during World War I, as well as by the tribe's desperate need to raise funds to cover the operating expenses of "their" new system.

In 1912, Crow Agent Evan Estep forwarded a petition from the Crow Business Committee to his superiors in Washington. The tribe's leaders had called for greater control over their own reservation administration, complaining that "the present system has [caused] the squandering of our lands and money perniciously, and the continuity of our stationary detriment."[23] Estep passed the document on with a chuckle. "Of course the whole proposition is absurd. . . . The time when the Crows will be able to manage their own affairs is not yet in sight." His reply symbolizes the stark contrast between the Crow community's sense of itself–both in 1912 and in the decades that followed–and the economic opportunities that lay before it. Adapting to their new reservation environment, Crow people had come to accept their permanent residence on a portion of their ancient homeland. Struggling with the authoritarian requirements of Indian Office officials and their minions, the tribe had preserved a measure of its dignity and many of its traditions. Faced with daunting enemies and weakened by declining numbers, they had produced leaders who weaved through their enemies' positions as briskly as their grandfathers had ridden among the Sioux and Blackfeet. But in their efforts to extend this emerging collection of national attributes to the management of reservation resources and commercial life, the Crows were circumscribed and excluded.

By the middle of the twentieth century, the Crows had learned that they could not be self-sufficient when they struggled to participate in the industrial economy. They understood that they could not reconcile the past and the present when the past meant economic independence and the present required dependence on those who stripped them of their wealth and offered them menial work at hourly wages in return. The result was an economic prospect characterized by rejection, exclusion, and contempt. Thus, the Crows, like their Northern Cheyenne neighbors, have struggled in recent decades to use the cultural and political strength they developed in the early years of this century to overcome the economic barriers that continue to surround them. In this way, they have shown themselves to be an undeniable presence in the Yellowstone valley, as well as worthy descendants of the tenacious, inventive people who first settled here thousands of years ago.

"No trees, no flowers, no, just hills and sagebrush, mountains. I thought it, I just couldn't take that. It was pretty hard to get used to after comin' from the city where there's lots of pretty trees and flowers, and walnut trees and hickory nuts and all of that, you know. . . . I couldn't get used to that. I just couldn't see where there was any greatness to bein' out here on the homestead." Lillian Stephenson

"They thought it was a king of jumpin' off place. They thought it, the men liked it better than the women. The men like this country. Because it was a lot of hunting and fishing, and they liked that. But of course it was tough country for the women . . . . Darn tough on women."
August Sobotka

"And go down on the Porcupine, it was flat. It looked great. Good fences on it, but it was no good. That gumbo when you plowed it, and the crop would come up nice, but you got a few hot days, and it just burned up. It was nothin'. So you had to, it was the worst down on the Little Porcupine and the Big Porcupine." Red Killen

"The railroad telling a big story, and showing pictures of fabulous trees with fruit, and fabulous fields with grain that was way up to their chest. You know, and well, the railroad just made a flowery picture of it. And where they took the pictures, I have no idea, because I'm sure they didn't get it locally." Birdie Streets

"The conditions of bringing this land into production is quite a story in itself. The land was covered—quite a lot of it—with native grasses and sagebrush and greasewood. A lot of the area had short sagebrush. You could plow that with a plow and cut it off pretty well. But the bigger sagebrush you had to grub with a grub hoe. . . . And we would, as youngsters, would pile sagebrush all day long, and then in the evening after schools, we would burn these piles of sagebrush. And all over the valley, you could see big fires of sagebrush being burned, and it was the height of ambition of the kids in school to see who could have the biggest bonfire that evening of sagebrush over the valley."
Charles Banderob

"And one of the things that's interesting, you know, we never knew a thing about this Northern Lights. Well, one night, my dad, I guess nature called him to go outside, you know. So he goes out and here he saw those Northern Lights . . . darn near half way across the horizon, and he said: 'Oh, oh. What in the world is this?' So and my mother, God bless her soul, she was very hysterical, she always very excitable, you know. . . . And the minute my mother saw those lights, she says: 'Oh, my God, the world is coming to an end. What in the world's goin' on?' Got us, all of us kids up and started praying. . . . Then my dad got to thinking. If this is fire, how come everybody around here is not excited? . . . So he told me to go see Mr. Halvor, see what he could tell us about it. . . . So we told him: 'What in the world is all this?' And he laughed. He says: 'Carranzas, go back to bed. Them are just Northern Lights.'" Santos Carranza

knowing our place: memory, history, and story in the yellowstone valley

barbara allen bogart

When people live in a place for any length of time, they come to know it in an intimate and complex way. Beyond the senses that wordlessly register the slope of the hills, the angle of the light, the weight of the wind, the voice of the river, the scents of the seasons, is knowledge of the place embedded in memories of particular moments and experiences. Those memories may be transmuted into stories told in conversations with friends and neighbors, over coffee or beer, at the dinner table or the cafe. Using stories as the common coin of social discourse, people share their experiences of place and thereby construct a collective understanding of their lives there. From that understanding, expressed in stories, past and present, oral and written, past and present, people weave their own history of place.

The people who arrived in the Yellowstone River Valley during the past century have created this kind of collective history for themselves. It is a different history than that of the native people. And it is different from the history outsiders construct, because it is told from the inside out; created from thousands of individual stories, it is intimate, personal, and communal. Each of the stories is necessarily unique, recounting a particular experience in a specific time and place. But the stories also resemble one another, like threads in a cloth. As the storytellers have spun and woven these story threads into the fabric of family and community history, they have created a tapestry that is rich in detail and color and that tells a single story of life in the valley as the people who live there see it.

The story that white residents of the Yellowstone River Valley tell themselves can be gleaned from published county and community histories, recounting events from initial white settlement through the recent past. Often compiled by local committees and produced for special occasions or anniversaries, such as the United States bicentennial or state or community centennials, these histories are community productions, containing biographical and autobiographical sketches; reminiscences and interviews; family, community, or neighborhood histories; and accounts of local institutions, including churches, schools, business, and clubs—all contributed by community members.[1]

Perusing one after another of these histories produces a sense of *deja vu*, for they are remarkably alike, not only in format but also in content. Regardless of a county's or community's idiosyncratic features, the histories exhibit strikingly similar patterns. For the reader, the overall effect is a sense that the history of the valley follows a single story line.

Arrival

The story begins with arrival in the new country. Individual stories describe people's initial responses to the valley, their early experiences in the place, and the transformations of identity that result from those experiences. Audie Cox, for instance, recalled moving to Montana as a young child:

I came to Big Horn County from Wyoming as a child of six. Mom had explained that we were leaving our home in Wyoming and going to the country in Montana. When we crossed the state line, she said, "Now we are in Montana." Somehow to my young mind it felt as though we were leaving the world behind. As I looked back, I said, "Goodbye, America, we're going to Montana."[2]

Another narrator was a little older than Cox when she arrived in the valley:

> We came to Montana in the spring of 1913 from Minneapolis. My dad came first and filed on land in the Pineview area. My mother and I followed as soon as a cabin had been built on our place.
>
> I was nine years old at the time, but I remember so well the night our train pulled into the station at Musselshell. My father was there to meet us. I soon got the scare of my young life as we had to ford the Musselshell River which was a raging torrent from the spring rains. As the horses were struggling through the water, pulling our laden lumber wagon, the eeriest howls pierced the air. Papa assured me they were from coyotes that were abundant in that country.[3]

In another story, a direct physical encounter with the new environment resulted in a changed appearance, which presaged an emerging new identity:

> When the immigrants, including the Thomases, finally reached their destination, they poured out of the wagons. The men set out to arrange the camp, while the women began to unpack their few remaining treasures from the Old World, pieces of furniture and family china that had miraculously escaped being broken during the long hard trek.
>
> While the adults were getting settled in, little Mary Ann Thomas decided to climb a pine tree to play scout. But when she climbed back down, she was covered with pitch. It had gotten in her hair, and she cried as her mother tried to comb it out. Finally it became clear that the only thing to do was to cut her hair—the beautiful black curls that had been the pride of her grandfather, whom they had left in Wales. He would certainly have disapproved had he seen his daughter and grandchildren, who had been brought up amid the charm of Old World customs, now living in the wild West.[4]

Another account of arrival and settlement focuses on a lost and found baby, somehow symbolic of the birth of new life in a new home:

> When the land around the Clark's Fork was opened for white settlement, a lot of people visited it ahead of the opening date to select their claims. One prospective settler, on a mission of this sort, shot an Indian in a quarrel over some timber. Apparently the settler had cut a pile of logs but the Indian had claimed them.
>
> The night of the killing, the Indians put on one of their customary dances of mourning. There were some twelve or fifteen other white people in the same area scouting for homesteads. These "Sooners" misinterpreted the death chant of the Indians

for a war dance and became alarmed and raced pell mell for the nearest ford across the Yellowstone which was near the east end of the White Horse Bottom. My uncle was part of this group.

Fording the river in the middle of a dark night could be uncertain and treacherous. One young couple in a light wagon had a young child. My uncle being on horseback was asked to carry the baby across the river in case the wagon was washed down the current in crossing. Uncle Joe could not find the family after the crossing, so he arrived at our home carrying a strange baby! The anxious parents were found the next morning.[5]

Adults as well as children underwent "baptisms" of one kind or another in their new home:

I came to Miles City in May, 1916, and soon filed my claim in the country south of there.

The first thing I did was to dig a well. I found lots of water at 11 feet. I didn't know but what I might starve, but I was not going to die for lack of water. The next thing I needed was lumber. I went to the Steadman mill and got some green lumber. I built the cabin but did not cover it. Then I left to work out till fall and by that time the lumber had dried and shrunk till the birds could fly in and out at will. So I put my bed in what was supposed to be my shelter and that night it poured down rain. All I had for protection was a table cloth made of oil cloth. I could not manage to stay dry as the rain came running off on all four sides into my bed.

A Mr. Gibbs had come out to my claim with me and set up a tent outside the cabin, so I just thought I'd go crawl in with him. But it was raining worse inside the tent than outside. So instead of starving on a government claim we came near drowning. That was my experience the first night on the claim.[6]

Arrival in the new home often produced culture shock:

When Blanche arrived from California in Cartersvllle, there were no buildings, just sagebrush and dust. They rolled her trunks down the dirty bank where she sat until the stage came. Three days later, after a long, dusty trip on a flat wagon, she arrived at the ranch. At barely eighteen, she was unprepared for this new life. There were men (but only an occasional woman), sagebrush, cactus, dirt and more dirt, and not a flower in sight. She cried and cried for people and California. Rollo put his arms around her and said, "Honey, if we can just stick out the three years to prove up on the homestead, I'll take you back." But in three years her roots were too deep; this was her home.[7]

The imagery of roots in this story is a powerful one. It suggests that those who transplanted themselves to the Yellowstone valley learned to adapt to local conditions in order to make it their home.

Coming to Terms with the Place

Once arrived in the valley, people discovered that living there was a difficult proposition. They coped with a hostile environment, they endured hard times, they faced dangers—real and imagined. In a new country, where everything is unknown and unfamiliar, fear can become the dominant emotional tone. In a number of stories from the Yellowstone valley, wild animals are the natural embodiment of danger:

An old man told me a true story that happened to a friend of his. He and a bunch of ranch hands were out rounding up cattle one day in the fall. When night came, one of the men didn't come back. Well, they couldn't go out to look for him because they knew there were grizzly bears around. Besides they were in the woods and it was really dark so they couldn't see anything anyway. Well, they found out the next morning that as the man was on his way back to camp, he came across a grizzly bear, so the man played dead. That's the only thing you can do with grizzly bears. Well, the grizzly bear stayed with him all night–he'd walk away and sit down for awhile, then come back and chew on him a little or maul him with his claw. Finally, towards morning, the bear left him and the man was able to crawl back to camp. Now this man had short cropped hair and when he got back to the camp, his hair had turned completely white.[8]

Sometimes unjustified fear led to foolish or embarrassing outcomes:

The land all looked so vast and scary that we didn't venture far from the house for the first few months. Once, later, growing more venturesome, we did get two or three hundred yards from the house when a ferocious looking animal rose up and looked at us over a downed log. We ran over each other getting to the house to tell about the "bear." Dad was not home so Mom took his old .44 six shooter and bravely marched up there, with kids trailing along, to scare it away; that was just too close to the house to have a bear parking. When we got back it was still there, but, believe it or not, it had shrunk til it looked exactly like a woodchuck.[9]

For the earliest white settlers, the potential for encounters with the native tribes present in the valley was equally anxiety producing. Stories of those encounters reveal vividly the attitudes of white settlers toward Indians, attitudes in which fear and contempt played equal parts:

Mrs. Bowles moved to Montana from West Virginia. She fell in love with Montana. She had a few uneasy times when the Indians were on the prowl, but there was no real trouble. Once two squaws came to their door asking for food and since it was advisable to give them what they asked for, she went to her pantry to get what she felt she could give them. She had left a huge bowl of boiled potatoes on the kitchen table and when she returned from the pantry, there were no potatoes in the bowl. She wondered what had happened, since it would have been impossible for the two Indian women to have eaten them in such a short time. As they left with the sack of food, one of them tripped, threw her arms up and out of her blanket came a hail of boiled potatoes. She gathered them up, dirt and all, stuffed them back in her blanket and they went on their way.[10]

According to another story, adults played a role in instilling unwarranted fear of Indians in their children:

My folks had been invited to Melvllle for Thanksgiving dinner. We kids were left home; I was eleven and the oldest of the five. In the afternoon there was a turkey shoot at Melville and we could hear the shooting very plainly, but had never heard of a turkey shoot and decided it was an Indian raid, as there had been rumors that the Indians on the reservation had been restless. So we hid out wherever we could find a place to hide; we even tied up our big dog so he wouldn't give us away. At first we hid in the straw stack but remembered hearing the Indians always burned all hay and straw stacks so out we moved and hid in tall grass and ditches.

Along in the afternoon a cowboy came along and we all came out to see who it was. After talking for a while my brother asked him if that was Indians shooting and he said, "Yes and you towheads better make yourselves scarce as there is nothing an Indian likes better than a towhead scalp." After he left we were more scared than ever. Two of my brothers lay under a dry cowhide hung over a fence all afternoon. The folks didn't get home until after dark and we hardly dared to come out even then.[11]

Among the most challenging elements of the valley's natural environment is the weather. Stories focus not so much on its harshness as on dangers it posed for humans. Rapid changes in weather, for instance, are a common theme in the stories:

One January in the 1920s there was a thunderstorm after nearly ninety degree weather. While I was going with my father to get firewood, the thunderstorm hit. The wind suddenly changed and it started to snow and got so bad that we had to stay at the cow camp at Rock Creek. By nightfall it was over thirty degrees below zero! We brought our wood home on a borrowed bobsled the next day.[12]

Even ordinary weather phenomena, such as wind, can play freakish tricks:

Mr. A. S. Shannon together with a man by the name of Mr. Hall ran the first drug store in Coulson, at that time all the stores being located in tents. Whenever a storm came up, he had to take all of his goods off the shelves and put them on the floor, so the flapping of the tent would not mix them. One day a big storm came up. Mr. Shannon took everything off the shelves and when the storm was over he put them all back. He had no sooner gotten them put back when another dust storm came up and before he could get them off the shelves again, a lot of them had gotten mixed. Shortly afterward a customer came into the store and asked for some flaxseed meal to make a poultice for his eyes. An hour later the customer came howling and lamenting into the store, saying that the flaxseed was hot and had burned his eyes out. This was not entirely true, although the flaxseed was indeed hot as it had been mixed with the Cayenne pepper during the dust storm.[13]

Unseasonable weather also extracts a more serious toll on human enterprises in these stories:

In 1912 the Cook brothers were wintering their cattle on the north side above the town of Custer. It was a hard winter and the boys had no opportunity to go to Billings. Then the weather turned nice in March, just about St. Patrick's Day, and Ernest and Edwin decided to get to town for supplies—enough to last them through calving season. Since there was no stage, train and no bus, they took two packhorses. Of course, the Montana weather obliged them. It turned cold with a bad snowstorm following. About dark on the tenth day, they returned to camp. When morning broke, they awakened to the sight of an empty feed yard and no cattle anywhere. What signs there were, were not good. The river had frozen over. The only open water was in the middle of the river. Evidently, the cows had started out on the ice to get water. They crowded each other and bunched up until the ice gave way. They lost them all![14]

In other stories, weather takes human life:

I recall one trip from Miles City to the SH ranch about sixty miles south. We were in a hurry because it looked like a big storm coming up. And did it ever storm. Rain, hail, thunder, and lightning. Two miles west of Ft. Keogh, just beyond where the road crossed to the south side of the N.P. track, lightning struck and knocked down several rods of Reservation fence. We hurried on in the mud.

On the west side of Lignite Creek, coming up the long hill we came to a team and wagon, stopped and off the road. The driver was dead, struck on top of the head by lightning. The dead man had on a yellow slicker and apparently had been standing up in the rain. He fell forward so the front wheel was against his jaw. The team wandered off the road and stopped. We left him as we found him with lines wrapped in hand. We unhitched the team, set the brake and tied them behind the wagon. We sent word through Horton station to the sheriff of Custer County. I never learned the man's name. He was working for the Mott ranch.[15]

A story of drowning in a flooded stream is made more poignant because it involves a mother and child:

> Mrs. Mercer was an excellent seamstress and was doing some sewing for Mrs. McNaney. It was late in the afternoon and she wanted to go home, but Bill McNaney tried to dissuade her because there had been a flash flood up the creek and Cabin Creek was bank full. She insisted that she had to go home, so Bill started out with her and her baby. In crossing Cabin Creek, the water was so deep that the horses started to swim. In the process of swimming the horses got their front feet over the neck yoke and began to flounder. Bill jumped to the bank and yelled for Mrs. Mercer to throw the baby to him. She wouldn't, and she, the baby, and the horses all drowned. The burial was on the north side of Cabin Creek.[16]

In this particular story, the woman's death—while lamentable—seems also partially attributable to her own stubborn insistence on ignoring the dangers posed by the weather. Many of these stories, while not fatalistic in tone, are at the very least stoic in their acceptance of a harsh and unyielding climate as one of the conditions for life in the Yellowstone River Valley.

Hard Times

The stories also tell of equally uncontrollable economic conditions that often combined with the weather to dash the dreams of a new and fruitful life in the valley. In this story, difficult conditions affect everyone in the community:

> It was during the deep depression in the ten years of no crops and the Montana dust bowl was a sorry place to live. I was the owner of a small drug store in Outlook, Montana. Every morning before I could open the store, I had to take a pitchfork and remove the Russian thistles from the door. One day one of the hardbitten ranchers drove up in front of the store and handed me an empty bottle to refill. In the back of his pickup I noticed two cases of eggs. When the farmer came back for his prescription later that afternoon, he still had the same two cases of eggs in his truck. I said, "What are you doing, Jim, giving those eggs a joyride?" The old settler said, "They would only give me five cents a dozen and I figured the wear and tear on the old hen was worth

more than that, so I'm going to feed them to the pigs."[17]

One especially moving story recounts the bitter end of their dreams for a group of ranchers:

> In the midst of the Depression, there were quite a lot of cattle left in the country but nothing at all for them to eat. The major companies in the east were glutted with western cattle and the railroad got so they would not carry any more cattle without a substantial down payment for freight. That's when the government had to step in and take the cattle off the farmer's hands. We had to trail them to Baker. About eight of us threw in together for the drive. I had close to 100 head, counting the calves. I had been ten years building up the herd. We sure were a sad and heavy-hearted group of men, knowing that the end of our cattle business was at hand. As we rode along slowly behind them, hardly anyone spoke. The same ache was in our heart and some of us felt like crying. I know I did.[18]

Occasionally during hard times, help came from unexpected quarters:

> After my father died in 1907, we saw very hard times. My mother dragged wood with a saddle horse and things like that. One time when she went hunting she shot a deer for food and it got up and ran over the hill. She went after it and ran smack into an Indian camp. They saw her and the deer and shot a couple of times. Mother lost no time getting home, putting us kids in the house, hanging blankets over the windows, barring the door and waiting, afraid to move. After a while she heard Indians outside, then all was quiet. After a while she peeked out and there was the deer all dressed out clean. They had been watching and knew there was a woman and kids alone.[19]

Accidents and Disasters

In addition to the threats posed by the natural environment, injury and loss of life from a variety of causes are commonplace in the stories. A number of stories deal with the risk posed by fire:

> Some people cutting wood had left a campfire burning and the wind caught it and drove it into the prairie. When he saw the smoke, Mr. Trunrud got what help he could and went to fight the fire. It was then three or four miles west of the ranch. The country at that time had lots of tall grass, making it hard to control, the fire being fanned by a very high wind. Mrs. Trunrud was left at the ranch with several children. She first went to the barn and turned out all the livestock, then saw that the wind was throwing burning debris onto the house. She started to the spring house carrying the eight-month-old baby and holding one of the younger children by the hand. The baby's hair caught on fire. She had to turn loose of the child she was leading to put out the fire

in the baby's hair. Then the child she was leading started to blow away and she had to catch her quickly before her clothes caught on fire.[20]

Even common activities like riding horseback could result in a life-threatening situation:

> In the very early days I remember a near tragedy that befell Bradley Jackson. He was beyond the east end of Lightning Creek, riding a not-too-gentle horse, when the horse fell. Bradley managed to get clear, but the horse stampeded and Bradley was left with a badly broken leg, miles from anyone. He became feverish. It was fully eight miles to the nearest water, a spring at the old Gus Hobbs place. Bradley began the arduous task of crawling on his hands and knees. After hours and hours he finally reached the spring. With survival uppermost in his mind, he thought of the only way to get help—start a fire. The creek was all cutbank. Painfully he burned a fire guard where the creek makes almost a U turn and then set the fire. The smoke was seen by the men who were riding from the East Fork Camp and in no time they were there. Bradley was placed on an improvised stretcher on a wagon and taken to town.[21]

A serious accident could have a dire impact on an entire family:

> A strip of coal lay at the foot of a high cutbank along Bloom Creek just a short distance from our house. One afternoon in January Howard was digging coal there for fuel when the bank caved in and covered him. I had just finished the lunch dishes and put the baby down for his nap. I told the two older children that I was going to talk to Papa for a minute and would be right back. I was always worried about that bank. After I found him, I run back to the house, told the children that I had to go for help, and warned them not to touch the fire or light a lamp. Then I hitched up the big draft horses to the lumber wagon—I was always afraid of them because of their size—and drove four miles to the Jacksons who had a phone. They heard the wagon coming, the horses running and someone screaming. I didn't realize I was screaming. I kept thinking that Howard would not like me to let the horses run because they were so big and heavy. They were white with frost with their breathing and sweating in the subzero temperature.
>
> It was dark by the time we got back to the homestead where the children were huddled in the dark, waiting.[22]

Neighbors

Calling on neighbors for help was a necessity when disaster threatened, and the neighborly duty to provide help is graphically described in this story:

The Crandalls moved out from Billings with three small children. The oldest, Ken, was five. They lived about fourteen miles north and a little east of Shepherd. He was out playing one afternoon and didn't come in when his mother called him to supper. So she went looking for him, searched until a few hours after dark. Mr. Crandall was in town at the time. It was in March and a cold wind was blowing. She ran to the nearest neighbors, half a mile away, but they weren't home. So she decided to go to the next neighbors, the Laceys, a mile and a half from her house. She blacked out when she got there, but when she recovered, begged them for help. So Claude Lacey set out on horseback and rode to all the neighbors, asking for help to find the boy. Someone got to our place about one in the morning. We went over on horseback to help the others who were coming from as far as thirty miles away. It was dark, cold and windy as hell.

We looked all that night for the boy. By morning over fifty people had come. We looked all that night and all the next day and through the second night. It was rough country with scrub pine and lots of cedar, gullies, dry creek beds and deep coulees. I went home to get my hounds. I thought they could find him where men on horses couldn't. I was riding along a high ridge when a fellow called out that he had found the boy. He was in the sagebrush dead. I carried him in the saddle until I came to a sheepherder's monument. I laid him down there and went down to a homestead for hot water and towels. He'd been in the sage and the wind had blowed sand in his face.

Mrs. Crandall spotted me on the way down with her boy. Two doctors had tried to give her a sedative but she had just kept walking and calling "Ken" so many times that her voice gave out. Her lips kept forming his name even when no sound came. I put the little boy in her arms. Her feet even in shoes were full of cactus.

Only one man out of all those asked refused to come. Neighbors them days used to borrow a lot from each other, help out. After people found out he wouldn't come, they avoided him and refused to borrow from him or lend to him.[23]

As this last story suggests, neighborliness was expected in times of trouble, but it was never taken for granted:

It was in November in 1921 that our homestead house burned. Dad built a fire in the cook stove and had filled the teakettle. Then both Mother and Dad went to do the milking. The two girls were still asleep in the bedroom. Ollie was soon to be married and Ruth was about twelve. All that could be figured out was that a gust of wind blew the front stove door opening, allowing hot coals to fall out on the kitchen floor. Ollie had the presence of mind to break out the bedroom window and the two girls got out, barefooted and in their nightgowns. Ruth was well nigh hysterical. Poor Ollie lost every stitch of her wedding trousseau, including her diamond ring.

Neighbors who saw the smoke were not long in coming. Before night scads of clothing and food had been delivered and good neighbors turned out to help the folks build the present house.[24]

Even small kindnesses were cherished:

Since our only way of getting around was horseback and there was no end to the work needing to be done, we didn't visit neighbors much, kept so much to ourselves, especially we women. One day Martha Lawrence came to our cabin driving an old wagon; she called me out. She had brought her greatest treasure, her sewing machine. Our first born was on his way and I had wondered how I'd ever prepare a supply of clothes for him. When Martha and I had carefully moved the machine from her wagon to my bit of earth, she drew open the drawers to show me lengths of lace and edgings, small buttons and fine thread. "I thought you could use these," she said.

"Yes," I bawled.[25]

But not everyone got along well with their neighbors, especially where ethnic prejudices existed or economic interests came into conflict:

Those first years at Plevna were a real trial. How I longed for the lush forests, roses, lilacs and huge ponds of my home in New Lustdorf, Russia. Here we only had coyotes, dust storms, thistles and the cattlemen who terrorized the new settlers. When my husband had left on an errand, I remember how they would come tearing up to the door of the shack, shooting their guns and yelling, scaring the children and me almost out of our wits. Never would I let on how frightened I was. They would scatter our small herds and whenever they pleased they would butcher one of the steers for themselves. One time they beat up my brother-in-law and left him to die. He crawled into a dry well and stayed there for two days before he crawled out and worked his way home.[26]

Not everyone turned the other cheek in the conflict with neighbors:

My mother's family came to Montana as homesteaders in 1916, including my great-grandmother. The first thing she did was to plant a garden on her half section, giving no thought to the fact that the vast unfenced grasslands in the area were grazed by the cattle of all the surrounding ranchers. When one of these cattlemen, Billy Glenn, passed by one day, he stopped to pay his respects. In making polite conversation with Great-Grandma, he asked her if she ran cattle. "I sure do," she explained. "Morning noon and night!"[27]

Measuring up to the Place

Judging from the stories, living in the Yellowstone valley called for special qualities. Ingenuity and resourcefulness in solving problems are particularly valued in the stories:

> One year when it was time to drive the Grosfield sheep to the railroad at Miles City, the camp tender telephoned A. M. [Grosfield] and said they had a terrible storm and he didn't know what to do. So A.M. took the train to Miles City. When he got there he went to the livery stable and asked to hire all their horses. He took the horses out to the sheep camp and asked the camp tender if he could find some rocks under the snow. A.M. had some gunny sacks along. He filled these with the rocks and tied them to the tails of the horses and he led them back to Miles City, making a wide trail with the dragging gunny sacks. The sheep followed and he loaded them on the railroad cars and shipped them back to Big Timber. It was said that A.M. was the only one who got out with his sheep and whole bands of sheep perished there that year.[28]

Nature couldn't always be outwitted, however. That's when, the stories suggest, it's best to admit when you're licked:

> The Hoppes were ranchers near Cinnibar. They had a good deal of trouble with elk in that vicinity. While Mr. Hoppe endeavored to protect the ranch from the devastations caused by the animals, he tried not to molest them, as some of the ranchers were doing. He and the ranch hands had built high fences around the hay stacks, using barbed wire and high poles, thinking they would keep out the elk. But repeatedly they would find their fences down, poles broke, and hay corrals harassed. One winter Mr. Hoppe conceived an idea to outwit the elk. It happened to be during the holiday season and quite in keeping with the season he and his men placed lighted lanterns on the haystacks. There was no danger of fire for several feet of snow lay on the ground and covered the stacks. It made a picturesque scene in the meadow. The family looked out upon it from the windows of the ranch house, confident of their success in frightening away their enemy.
>
> The family retired but Walter was prompted about midnight to look out once more. The elk were not satisfied by such simple Yuletide decorations. They too would add their bit. Here they were, a bunch of them, loping over the meadows in grand style with the lanterns hooked over their horns. It was New Year's night and another year of victory to the elk was being ushered in. Right there Walter made his New Year's resolution: that was to sell out.[29]

Toughness and that ineffable quality that westerners call grit were perhaps the most highly prized traits in valley folks, according to their stories:

My grandfather had heard of a small bunch of cattle that had not been shipped in the fall because the owner had broken his leg. He found the place and asked the owner if he had these cattle in, that he was interested in buying them. The old man said he had the cattle, but that they had been turned out for the winter. He thought, though, that his wife, a woman of fifty-odd years, could find them. Supposing that the man meant to send her horseback, my grandfather rode on the next place, promising to come back that night.

He returned about 9 o'clock in the evening, by which time the temperature had dropped to around thirty below. He found that the wife had not yet returned, and immediately became convinced in his mind that she had frozen to death. The old man, however, was not worried, insisting that "she's a pretty good woman."

About eleven that night, the old woman returned, with all 25 head of cattle, on foot. She explained that she had not found the cattle till almost noon, and that they were mixed with range cattle. By the time she had gotten them separated (still on foot) it had been dark; she then drove them to the place. She seemed to think little of the experience but my grandfather was speechless.[30]

Learning to Laugh

In the face of the conditions under which they lived and the dangers they encountered, it is little wonder that people often resorted to laughter as a coping device. Some stories play off fears and apprehensions:

One summer in Elliston, Sam was watching some Indians, who had camped there overnight, load up their wagons preparatory to moving on. A neighbor came by and asked the Indian if he'd like another boy. "Sure" came the answer. So the neighbor grabbed Sam and threw him on top of the wagon. Sam said he was never so scared in all his life, but when he scrambled off the wagon in a hurry and hightailed it back home, he heard the Indian and the neighbor roaring with laughter.[31]

Other stories revolve around the laughable actions of individuals:

The main method of getting to Billings, other than horse and wagon, was on the "Dinky," a Northern Pacific mini-train with a baggage and passenger car. The time schedule of the Dinky didn't always fit, as one homesteader, Tom Makinson, found out. His business necessitated his catching a late night train to Ballantine. Then he struck out on foot, but lost his bearings as the night was so dark, and ended up at Spec Smith's place. It didn't take Spec's dogs long to put Tom up a tree and he began yelling "Where am I? Where am I?" This woke Spec up and he poked his head out the door and said, "You damn fool, you're up a tree!"[32]

The apparently universal theme of foolish questions also shows up in the Yellowstone valley, adapted to local conditions:

The greatest change was when the REA came in somewhere around 1940. The REA put a notice in the Hysham *Echo* that the electricity would be turned on at 2:30 on a given Monday morning. My wife at that time worked at the REA office. Someone from Sarpy called in and said, "If you turned the electricity on at 2:30, what time will it get up here?"[33]

Finally, even humorous stories are used to make a point about the Yellowstone River Valley as home to the people who settled there, raised their families, and made a life for themselves.

In the spring of 1916, the Hays' first child was born. Susie wanted to deliver her baby at home, but the responsibility of serving as midwife in lieu of a doctor frightened her sister-in-law Mary and she coaxed Susie to go to Forsyth for proper care. A mare in the team of horses was ready to foal and Susie couldn't decide whether she or the mare was worse off, especially when Pudge [her husband] started whipping the team to race the stork the last part of the 40-mile trip. When they finally reached Forsyth, their regular doctor was out on a call. By the time Pudge returned with the only doctor he could locate, Susie had delivered the baby alone.

      Before time for her next baby to be born in the spring of 1918, Susie made sure in advance that a neighbor, Mrs. Pope, would care for her at the ranch. When the little girl was born and Pudge named her Montana, another neighbor asked him what he would have named the child if it had been a boy. Pudge replied without a trace of a grin, "Yellowstone."[34]

So the story ends with the transformation of a strange and unfamiliar place into home and with the shaping of identity around the place. Comprising thousands of individual narratives, the story goes something like this:

(1) We came here from somewhere else. Sometimes we came alone, sometimes with family. We arrived as children and as adults, as men looking for land and work, as women to teach school or join our husbands.

(2) Our new home was unfamiliar and full of frightening elements.

(3) Once here, we built homes and started families. As children, we remember playing with our brothers and sisters, neighbors and schoolmates, exploring the world around us with its wonders and its dangers. As adults, we recall hard work and hard times, economic struggle and emotional hardship.

(4) We contended with bitter cold and snow, floods and drought. The weather was extreme and apt to shift suddenly and unexpectedly, doubling the hazards to our lives and efforts.

(5) Survival was a constant struggle. Accidents and natural disasters threatened and sometimes took the lives of our families and friends.

(6) In this struggle we relied on one another by trading work, aiding in illness and death, sharing food and goods, helping rebuild. We still remember individual acts or breaches of neighborliness.

(7) Dealing with the difficulties that the place handed out called for ingenuity and grit.

(8) Even when times were hard, we took time to laugh.

(9) The valley made us what we are today.

Thus, the stories told here, along with the hundreds like them that appear in county and community histories from the Yellowstone valley, have meaning on at least two levels. For the individual storytellers, the stories link the valley's past with life there in the present: This is where the bank caved in, where the mother drowned with her baby, where the wagon overturned, where I saw the bear. The stories of one's own experiences, linked with the stories of others', become a kind of experiential geography of the valley.

The stories also have meaning on a collective level as well by ratifying recognizable kinds of experience—migration, hardship, neighborliness, grit—as significant elements of local history and local character. Individuals can then situate their personal experiences within this collectively constructed understanding of the valley's past, an understanding that takes the form of a narrative—the story that comprises all their stories. Through the interplay of these individual stories with the collective story, residents of the valley come to know their home place and its history, to perceive their own experiences as fitting into the larger historical experience of the Yellowstone River Valley, and, in so doing, come to feel in a powerful way that they belong to the place.

dreamers of horses

mary clearman blew

Theo's Butte juts out of the rims under the South Moccasin mountains of central Montana, familiar as a sentinel, its striated sandstone cliffs frowning down across the slope and the blue stretch of benchlands on the far side of the deep Judith River gorge. I don't know if anyone still calls the butte Theo's. It has been thirty years since my great uncle owned the land and farmed around the base of the butte, though summerfallow still runs up the slope, as steep as modern farm equipment can be towed, toward the abrupt cliffs and the crown of jackpines that can be seen for miles.

Theo's Butte has been the subject of legends from the first years that my family lived within its shadow, starting in 1882. Someone knew someone who had collected a Mason jar full of Indian beads from the butte. Other stories told of lost caches of Indian artifacts, and how a man who worked for Theo had explored one of those cracks in the cliffs and found beaded saddles and weapons and beautiful clothing, but by the time he came back with ropes and a shovel, a landslide had buried the treasure cache—*it's still buried up there, somewhere.*

Crow Indians were said to have been camped at the mouth of the Little Judith River when they were stricken by an epidemic of smallpox. Parents, so the account went, carried their dead children up to the butte and left their bodies in the deep crevices in the sandstones. Years later my great-grandmother was afraid to let her children play on those cliffs because she thought that living smallpox germs might still lie in wait in the dark places. At least one unmarked grave is said to have left its depressed oblong in the sod on top of the butte. *It was a fight that broke out over a card game—no, it was a fight over water rights*—and the man who was killed was buried on the spot. But the older women in my family tell a different story, about a stillborn baby handed to its young father who, penniless and bewildered, wrapped it in a quilt and carried it up to the butte and buried it above the rimrocks before he rejoined his outfit and went overseas in 1942.

I remember only once, when I was ten or so, being taken to a family picnic on Theo's Butte, and I remember how our ranch trucks and the heavy cars of the California uncles lumbered over the ruts and boulders of the old wagon road that wound up behind the rimrocks, and my surprise to discover that the top of the butte, which looked so flat and even from the remote distance, was as rough and gullied and grassgrown as ordinary prairie when I jumped down from the bed of the truck to find my footing after the jolting ride. The men lifted down watermelons and cases of pop and beer. The mothers complained about the lack of water, but they started a dry camp and found a level place in the shade of jackpines to spread blankets and set out the food. When we cousins ran off to explore, they warned us, not about landslides or lingering smallpox germs or small stillborn ghosts, but about the rattlesnakes that denned down in the rimrocks and crawled out to sun themselves on the crumbling ledges of soft, gritty stone.

I was born into an illusion of permanence. Names of landmarks were as certain as the blue line of the butte itself. The Grandma's Trees, the Sheepshed Bottom, the Water Coulee. Pigweed grew up through the piles of rotting logs that had been Carrie's homestead cabin, Gobbie's homestead cabin, Bess's homestead cabin. Every cattle trail, every river ford had its story—*that's the hole in the crick where the roan colt drowned—that's the piece where the grassfire burned almost as far as the granary*—and all the stories were ours, about a private landscape that had taken one family a hundred years to claim and put down roots into, to leave and die.

But that landscape must have seemed very different to my great-grandmother when she laid eyes on it for the first time. She had left Pennsylvania and the shade of ancient hardwood trees to travel west by train and stagecoach to join her husband in the Montana Territory, and the only stories of place she knew were the ones she had read in his letters. An empty land waiting to be transformed, he wrote. Rich in resources: grass, water, timber. Good winter feed and shelter for livestock. As ranchers they would make their fortune. And so she jolted deeper into the dry haze with her fourteen-month-old son in her arms and came at last to a cabin in the sagebrush. She began almost at once to rehearse the stories she would pass on to her children about her first years on the homestead.

My great-grandfather's way of facing the unknown was to transform it. His stories had been about the west as an adventure; he saw himself as protagonist, pitted against weather and a stubborn landscape that he had to wrestle into square miles with his surveyor's stakes and chains. But her stories were about disasters averted by the narrowest of margins. Berrying with her children and stumbling into a den of rattlesnakes. Scaring a herd of cattle away from her cabin by firing at them with a 10-gauge shotgun that knocked her flat with its recoil. Innocently giving directions to the man who drove up to her door with a team and a covered wagon; when it turned out that he was a killer, hauling the bodies of his victims to the river where he buried them in a gravel bar, she supposed it had been only her luck that kept him from adding her and her children to the load in his wagon.

Stories are a way of explaining the inexplicable, of giving shape to that which has no shape, meaning to that which eludes meaning. Without stories, the first white venturers into the west saw space without end, indescribable

lights and shadows, unfamiliar beasts and men. The earliest painters in the
west struggled with the same amorphousness; we can see in the works of
Bierstadt, Audubon, Bodmer, how they were bewildered by western
landscape, how they brought their European comparisons with them to tell
them what they were seeing. And, in the earliest settlers' narratives, we can
read about the terror of boundlessness.

Nannie Alderson, who left a soft plantation life in West Virginia for
her husband's cattle ranch in eastern Montana in 1883, the same year my
great-grandmother left Pennsylvania for central Montana, reflected on her
fears a half century later and wondered if she had gone crazy with isolation.
"I was haunted by a demon of fear," Nannie tried to explain to Helena
Huntington Smith, who wrote down her story. "I can't remember when it
began to grow on me, but I know that until I lived on Muddy I had never
been afraid except those few times I was left alone. For the most part I never
had sense enough to be scared, even when there was something to be scared
of, such as a tribe of hostile Indians all around us. But now I was nervous
about one thing or another all the time.[1]

Unfortunately, Helena Huntington Smith, taking notes, heard the
story she was prepared to hear and saw what she was prepared to see: "you
would never guess [Nannie] was a pioneer woman except for something
about her eyes. They look at you very straight, without flinching. Few
women reared in luxury have eyes like that. . . .[2] And so *A Bride Goes West*
becomes a curious double narrative of the intrepid woman Helena
Huntington Smith superimposed upon the terrified woman Nannie
Alderson knew she was. Terrified of what? Nannie never was able to
articulate her fear, even to herself, but she knew it focused upon her
husband's horses, and she knew it was not completely without a rational
basis, for the stallions were so powerful and so violent that her husband
carried a revolver when he rode after them.

Finally it did happen, this thing I dreaded, and I was there to see it . . .
on the same impulse, as it seemed, the two great horses made a rush and each
one broke through his gate at the same instant as though it were pasteboard.
They met in the center, where they reared and fought like bloodthirsty wild
beasts or like the horses in nightmares, pawing and tearing at each other's
throats. The men were all there, with axes in their hands, but it seemed

minutes before they could stop them. Before the battle was over the ugly gray had whirled and kicked, and the brown who was gentle to humans had caught the other's pastern in his teeth and had bitten clear through the tendons, leaving him a cripple for the rest of his life.[3]

The horses in nightmares. My great-grandmother would have heard this story in a way Helena Huntington Smith could not, for it tells about a loss of control, about force run rampant across a landscape where all previous points of reference have failed. Nannie had brought with her a set of assumptions about the Montana Territory. She had thought she and her husband would make their fortunes quickly there. She had expected to find freedom from trifling social restraints. She never saw the contradiction in her blithe expectation that the social structures of the agrarian south would follow her wherever she went and keep her safe, that gentility mattered, that noblesse would oblige, and that the Northern Cheyennes would, somehow, accept her relegation of them to the familiar and comforting role of the "darkies" she had known in West Virginia. But her terror deepened as the safety net of her assumptions dissolved.

Eventually Nannie's worst nightmare was realized when her husband was kicked to death by one of the horses, although by that time the Aldersons had left the ranch for the relative shelter of Miles City. How could she explain to Helena Huntington Smith that she refused ever again to live out of calling distance of children or neighbors? How could she, or my great-grandmother, explain to anyone the threat of an empty horizon? How could they explain the terror of meaninglessness? By the time the children were old enough to listen, they could not hear what the white women of the first generation in Montana were trying to say.

Instead they idealized them. The following is how one of her sons concludes his profile of his parents, my great-grandparents:

> During this discourse little mention has been made of my Mother. While she had no direct part in the building of tunnels and ditches and houses and other similar jobs, you can believe she had a vital role in all the activities of her family. She was my fathers [*sic*] guiding light as he was her shining knight. This is not said in levity but in earnest sincerity. . . . A book would be too brief to relate all the accidents and near tragedies that took place on our ranch. Our Mother stood up to all of them. Again I could write a book about our Mother, and her children. Instead, I will simply say that Mother's children adored her.[4]

What would that unwritten book have contained? Except for the fragments of her terror, my great-grandmother's narrative has been erased, as has, in many ways, her husband's narrative of transformation and prosperity. The Montana story that has taken its place, from our perspective in the waning years of the twentieth century, is A.B. Guthrie, Jr.'s, whose six major novels trace the history of white settlement in Montana from the heyday of the beaver trade in the early nineteenth century through the opening of the Oregon Trail and the development of the great cattle empires in the 1880s up to the great homestead movement of the early twentieth century and the advent of the second world war. The Montana of *The Big Sky* is an undefiled wilderness, described as an earthly paradise in the eyes of the white mountain men who are drawn by its beauty and its promise of freedom from the restraints and corruption of civilization, where the natural grandeur of mountains, streams, and prairie is enjoyed by the Blackfeet. The paradise is doomed, for the mountain men carry the seeds of its destruction within them. Every man of them, Guthrie emphasizes again and again, kills the thing he loves. Boone and Jim and Dick Summers wipe out the beaver, they infect the Indians with whisky and syphilis, and they open a trail for white settlers and their families.

> A passel of 'em's went a'ready, and more's a-comin'. . . . I reckon they'll
> be trompin' over the trails we made and climbin' the passes you and
> me saw first and pokin' plows in along the river bottoms where we
> used to camp. They got a hunger, they have. This nigger don't look for
> the old days to come back.[5]

In *The Way West,* Dick Summers's prophesy is fulfilled; the Evanses endure every hardship in their quest for fresh new farmland and freedom, but their dream, too, is doomed; they, too, kill what they love. By the opening pages of the next novel, *These Thousand Hills,* an Evans grandson, Lat, looks at the overworked hills of Oregon and sees crowded faces and a filthy river:

> It was good and lonely water once, the Umatilla was, before people
> had begun coming in to spoil it, bringing plows to rip up pastures and
> cattle to graze ranges already overgrazed and sheep to make affairs
> still worse. That was the trouble with all Oregon, here and elsewhere
> even more—too many people, too much stock, too many homestead
> claims, and so wild life was disappearing and cows were poor in flesh
> and price, and streams ran tame and clouded.[6]

What can Lat Evans do but sign on with one of the cattle outfits and ride into the "thousand hills" of northern Montana in search of the new beginning that eluded his parents and grandparents? Gradually, of course, his youth and zest give way to disillusionment and loss as he pays the price of existence. At least in *Arfive,* set in small-town Montana in the early years of the twentieth century, the main characters know from the very beginning that they are seeing the end of life as they knew it. The Arfive school board that hires Professor Collingsworth is uneasy about the change which his presence will bring. "The winds are blowing. . . . The preacher and the schoolmaster are harbingers, and homesteaders will hasten the change."[7] Collingsworth himself, after talking about the past with an old fur trapper, understands that he is helping to bring about a not wholly desirable future:

> People would come seeking homesites. The straggling forerunners, indeed, were already coming, bringing plows and grains and garden stuff and hope and the seed of their loins. When there were enough of them, what would be left? What of the old times of uncluttered acres, of hope that no homesteader would hope for, of blithe and unstudied assurance? . . . Here, as schoolteacher and even as churchman, he felt a touch of discomfort, for he was part as well as agent of change.[8]

What he does not understand is the consequences for himself, for Collingsworth as surely as Boone Caudill carries the seeds of destruction within himself. Ultimately Collingsworth, too, kills what he loves, his wife May, who dies from overwork and too many pregnancies. And in *Arfive*'s sequel, *The Last Valley,* Collingsworth's daughter and her husband must try to deal with social, political, and environmental issues grown to crises by the irresponsibilities of the past. Guthrie lets no one off the hook, from mountain man to pioneer schoolmaster. The history of the westward movement has been a series of aggression in the name of freedom and opportunity: aggression against the land, against the Blackfeet, against women like Teal Eye and Callie and May Collingsworth, and finally against the future, as Guthrie, drawn himself to the dream of idyllic splendor in the mountains, hammers down his lesson. *Every man kills what he loves.* And yet even in Guthrie's apocalyptic vision lies the implication of control. Kill it, dominate it, manage it, ride it with Spanish spurs and a spade bit, but control it before it controls you.

Landscape in Montana literature often is treated as character, as protagonist or antagonist. My great-grandfather's notes reverberate with descriptions of central Montana. How he loves this place! Fresh water, trout, mountains, prairies, wild game. But he never doubts his task of surveying and measuring landscape and converting it into property. He never questions the economic and political policies that brought him west as an engineer for the Great Northern Railway. Place becomes opportunity, his wife becomes his idealized "guiding light," and the culture he has replaced must be re-imagined from noble savage to degraded and unredeemable man in his lowest common denominator:

> . . . away they drift, these conquerors of the coyote and wolf,
> alternately gorging and starving, against whom the white man has
> "sinned" in killing off the buffalo thus removing their "feast"
> without effort.[9]

Selecting one narrative means discarding other possibilities. Faces are crowded to the margins, screams can't be heard. When Montana's first Native American novelist, D'Arcy McNickle, submitted his draft of *Wind from an Enemy Sky* to an eastern publisher in 1936, he was told it wasn't "Indian" enough. Neither degraded nor idealized, McNickle's characters affirm their tribal past as a source of present power. With forgetting comes a terror like that which waited for Nannie Alderson in her dreams, or for my great-grandmother in the unfamiliar sandstone rims of the butte that was not yet called Theo's after the second of her sons. Old Catherine in *The Surrounded* lives to discover that

> . . . now in old age she looked upon a chaotic world–so many things
> dead, so many words for which she knew no meaning. . . . How was it
> that when one day was like another there should be, at the end of
> many days, a world of confusion and dread and emptiness?[10]

In meaninglessness is disintegration. But in remembering the old stories, honoring the old customs, aware of themselves as a people through their tribal connections with past and present, contemporary native American writers are finding the potential for narratives that seemed doomed when told by white writers. In these narratives, the past is not something that must be escaped; rather, it must be sought out. The inexorability of Guthrie's vision of destruction is transformed in the telling by James Welch, whose characters find in landscape an acknowledgement of self that is almost transcendental in tone. Welch's Indian lawyer recognizes place not as protagonist or antagonist in relation to himself, but as integral to himself:

> To him, the country was not empty, but remote and secluded, even intimate if you were alone. . . . Many times when he was far away, Sylvester had envisioned these plains, the rolling hills, the ravines, the cutbanks and alkali lakes, the reservoirs and scrublands, and he always saw life. He saw a hawk circling over a prairie dog town. He saw antelope gliding through, over and under fences at a dead run. He saw a rattlesnake sleeping on a warm rock, or coiled, tongue flicking, tail rattling, as it slowly undulated back away. He saw beauty in these creatures and he had quit trying to explain why. It was enough to hold these plains in his memory and it was enough to come back to them.[11]

The plains are neither ally nor adversary for Sylvester Yellow Calf, but part of a beautifully ordered system which includes him as surely as it does the hawk or the rattlesnake. He can fuse back with the whole if he can let go of his separate sense of himself. *Getting and spending, we lay waste our powers–little we see in Nature that is ours*–Sylvester, who separated himself from the Blackfeet reservation via basketball scholarships, law school, and a budding political career, who now finds himself unable to form connections either with whites or with Indians, could be taking advice from Wordsworth; except that, unlike Wordsworth, he doesn't yearn for glimpses of perished divinity. For Sylvester, briefly, his merging with the beautiful system is sufficient in itself. And yet what is more terrifying than personal annihilation? Rarely in literature written by white Montanans is the system sufficient in itself. Ivan Doig's McGaskill novels can be read as a gradually learned stewardship of the land, culminating when, in *Ride with Me, Mariah Montana*, an aging Jick McGaskill deeds the family ranch to the Nature Conservancy. Norman Maclean concludes his famous novella in *A River Runs Through It* with the lovely passage on the implicit word of God he hears under the sound of water in the Blackfoot River:

> Eventually, all things merge into one, and a river runs through it. The river was cut by the world's great flood and runs over rocks from the basement of time. On some of the rocks are timeless raindrops. Under

the rocks are the words, and some of the words are theirs.

I am haunted by waters.[12]

William Bevis has said, in connection with *A River Runs Through It,* that either the universe is a chaos of natural phenomena, out of which we wring meaning, or it is itself meaningful, based on a design or logos that precedes material creation.[13] *Logos:* the Word, which is the beginning, which is God. As his Presbyterian father insists, Maclean can hear the words under the water which precede the creation of the river if he listens for them. Then "all existence fades to a being with my soul and memories and the sounds of the Big Blackfoot River and a four-count rhythm and the hope that a fish will rise, "[14] and, as surely as the Indian lawyer, although on terms completely different from his, private but profound, Maclean fuses with the beautiful system.

Where will most of us find meaning? Not in Manifest Destiny, not in the promise of the westward movement, not in romantic despair. Perhaps not in Maclean's Presbyterian salvation, probably not in tribalism, for too few of us can find these connections. In letting go of one story, we risk the abyss until we can find another. The distance between the rattlesnakes in the rimrocks that my mother warned me about and the rattlesnakes which Welch's Indian lawyer sees on his drive through northern Montana that sun themselves and undulate back from the highway is nearly immeasurable. And yet some of the new narratives try to measure that distance. Ruth McLaughlin, who grew up in eastern Montana, concludes one of her short stories with the following passage:

His mother stands on the front step and thinks of the children. . . . Far away beyond the blank of the wheat fields she sees something begin to move. It is grey and writhes. It is probably the dust of the mailman, but it could be the start of a cloud. She remembers when she had first come to Montana, it was just at the end of the war. The train had dropped her down from the mountains of the west coast onto the plains on the same day the bomb had fallen on Hiroshima. Weeks later, she had seen newsreels of it at the theater. That night, held in her new husband's arms, she had listened to her first thunderstorm in this new country; the sky crashed as though it would break and fall. She imagined the cows and horses in the pasture beginning to move at the first sounds of thunder, pressing into a herd, running faster now for shelter . . . but there was no place to run to.

There were no trees, no shelters, no mountains where the plain ended
where one could lean against and wait it out. She learned later that
though they knew there was no shelter they raced anyway, tried to
escape, pressed on together in the dark barely sensing in time where
they might stumble; leaving behind them all the space that was
dangerous, moving into some promise that was slightly ahead
of them.[15]

A shift has taken place, the unwritten book is opening. What my
great-grandmother sensed is now out in the open. For McLaughlin, the
terror is no longer in landscape. At some point the women have realized that,
if each man kills what he loves, they are among the targets. Women's faces,
Indians' faces, have been crowded to the mountains; their voices have been
silenced with the sound of the rivers and the eloquent eyes of animals.
McLaughlin's horses are no longer Nannie Alderson's horses of nightmare,
but sensate creatures like herself, knowing no shelter but racing to escape the
external threat of annihilation. Her ranch wife doesn't fear the horses, she
fears with the horses. But she won't accept disintegration. Knowing that hers
is one of the faces on the margins, feeling what the horses feel, she will run
the risk of her own narrative.

Ripley Schemm writes,

I know those stones asleep in my dream of prairie sky. Ice of a million
winds ago melted down their flanks, left them roaming wild
bunchgrass, some turned piebald with lichen, some scarrred by storm.
Let it be danger of rattler or rusted tine near your foot that wakes
them. Horses watch in their sleep. They rise and bolt for the ridge.[16]

"Life is motion," writes Annick Smith. "Choose love. A person can fall
in love with horses."[17] Listen for other, younger voices. In the next few years
they will erupt in a flood.

One autumn day in Albuquerque I listened to the Navajo poet Luci
Tapahansa explain Dine mythology and its connection to landscape, and I
realized that, for her, the rocks and cliffs of the Southwest were underpinned
by a system of order which preceded creation, and that, furthermore, this
system of order was understood and accepted by a whole people. In contrast,
my own ways of ordering were private and tenuous. A year ago my cousin Joe
Murray had taken my sister Jackie and me on a visit to our old ranch, which

had been my great-grandfather's ranch. Joe met us on the dirt crossroad where the mailboxes had been and drove us in his four-wheel-drive outfit down the old hill. For Jackie it was an excursion into the unfamiliar. She had left this place when she was two years old. For me it had the unreality of a recurring dream. Nothing was as it had been.

Joe pointed out the cutbank where, one spring morning fifty years ago, he had found the sick horses. "I'd saddled Lucy and ridden out after breakfast to bring them in. When I found them, I didn't know what was the matter with them. They could hardly walk. I didn't think I'd ever get them up that trail to the corral, she was so dizzy. That was the first we saw of the sleeping sickness."

One cutbank, another cutbank, exactly alike. Across a sagebrush slope, cutting across coulees in a line as exact and straight as a ruler, aiming across country for Theo's Butte with the precision of an arrow shot, was the remains of a fence. Ancient cedar posts, set to last a hundred years. Rusted barbed wire, sagging off its staples. In its exactitude was its dominance. For a few more years that straight line was going to be imposed across shortgrass and sandstone.

"The old line fence," said Joe. And I understood that this was the boundary between my great-grandfather's original ranch and his oldest son's, my grandfather's.

"Who built it, do you think?" I asked.

Joe ruminated for a moment, then shook his head and laughed softly as he understood the question behind my question. "Albert, probably," he said. Albert was my grandfather, dead years before I ever was born. Legends reverberated around his name. Albert, the man of calm, the top hand, the fiddle player and blacksmith and breaker of horses. He was larger than life. And now here were these cedar posts, gnarled by the years and set by his hands in their inexorable straight march across landscape toward the butte. Joe and I were silent. I knew the associations were flooding him as they were me. I also knew that our associations were private, that he and I were perhaps the last left alive to sense the meaning of that fence. Even my sister could only feel the silence. For the fence gave no meaning to landscape; the fence was a superimposition, a ghost of order, more tenuous in spite of the strength of its cedar than the thin soil and the sparse grasses it was set in.

For comfort, I thought of the horses of nightmares, and of the horses Joe Murray remembered, and then of Annick's horses, and of Ripley's boulders like sleeping horses, and of Ruth's horses, running from the thunder toward the promise that lies slightly ahead. In the illusion of permanence, words remain.

Plate A
Broom Exhibit for the Yellowstone County Fair
Billings, Montana
1894
Western Heritage Center

Plate B
Barracks
Fort Custer, Montana
1877
Western Heritage Center

Plate C
Steamboat Expansion
Yellowstone River between Mondak and Glendive
1907
MonDak Heritage Center

Plate D
German Russian Picnic
Eastern Montana
1913
Evelyn J. Cameron, Photographer
Montana Historical Society

Plate E
Burning Sagebrush to Clear the Land
Huntley, Montana
ca. 1910
National Archives

Plate F
Gebo Mine
Bridger, Montana
1900
Western Heritage Center

Plate G
Construction of the Lower Yellowstone Irrigation Project
Intake, Montana
1905
National Archives

Plate H
Northern Cheyenne Chief Two Moons with Women in Front of Sam O'Connel's Store
1900
Lame Deer, Montana
Montana Historical Society

Plate I
Dudes at the OTO Guest Ranch
Paradise Valley
1938
Courtesy Clara Bell Bounine
Western Heritage Center

Plate J
Tourists at Yellowstone National Park
Mammoth, Wyoming
Early 1900s
National Archives

Plate K
Land Office
Judith Gap, Montana
ca. 1910
Courtesy John Bills
Western Heritage Center

Plate L
Fourth of July Picnic
16 Mile Bench
1911
Western Heritage Center

Plate M
H. J. Hoppe's Ranch
Upper Yellowstone Valley
1885
Gardner, Montana Territory
Haynes Foundation
Montana Historical Society

Plate N
Indian Family Going to Crow Agency to the Annual Fair
Crow Agency, Montana
1941
Marion Post Wolcott, Photographer
Library of Congress

Plate O
Mexican–American Sugar Beet Worker
Hysham, Montana
1939
Arthur Rothstein, Photographer
Library of Congress

imagining montana: photographs by frank j. haynes, l.a. huffman, and evelyn cameron

john r. peters-campbell

"The plains . . . are grasslands. Their vast expanse flows for many hundreds of miles . . . and sweeps inland to the dead heart of the continent. In a good season, if the eyes are turned to the earth on those plains, they see a tapestry of delicate life—not the luxuriant design of a book of hours by any means, but a tapestry nonetheless, designed by a spare modern artist."

On the plains, the earth meets the sky in a sharp black line so regular
that it seems as though drawn by a creator interested more in
geometry than the hills and valleys of the Old Testament. Human
purposes are dwarfed by such a blank horizon. . . . Its blankness
travels with our every step. . . . Because we have very few reference
points on the spare earth, we seem to creep over it, one tiny point of
consciousness between the empty earth and the overarching sky.
Because of the flatness, contrasts are in a strange scale. A scarlet
sunset will highlight grey-yellow tussocks of grass as though they
were trees. Thunderclouds will mount thousands of feet above one
stunted tree in the foreground. A horseback rider on the horizon will
seem to rise up and emerge from the clouds.[1]

The words are those of a woman remembering her childhood place in
the Western Outback of Australia in the early part of this century. But they
echo those of many women and men living alone in the midst of land like
what Miles City photographer L.A. Huffman and his neighbors called the
"Big Open."[2] Huffman and Evelyn Cameron were two outsiders who settled
in the country along the Yellowstone River east of Billings after the 1871
congressional decision to deny Native American sovereignty. Through the
relatively inexpensive and portable medium of photography, they worked
hard to redefine the Yellowstone for themselves, their communities, and
other outsiders. Frank Jay Haynes, another outsider, brought his photography
business to the Yellowstone valley along the route of the Northern Pacific
Railroad to inform and attract people from outside the region.

Photography took the place of painting as the source of authoritative
images of the West in the years around the turn of the century. This was in
keeping with the changing taste of the American public after the Civil War
and the dramatic advance of technology. Since the American Revolution,
painting had been the authoritative media for public, visual communication.
Landscapes by artists such as Albert Bierstadt (1830-1902) and Thomas
Moran (1837-1926) created metaphors out of specific places (Wyoming's
Wind River Range and the Grand Canyon of the Yellowstone, for example)
that came to represent the character of the larger West for the art-buying
public in the East, where explorers, travellers, and prospective settlers lived.[3]

Photography, at first, fulfilled a different role. What had begun as a
means of dispassionately recording events in the Civil War, as in photographs
by Alexander Gardner (1821-1882), or authenticating scientific work, as in

the exploration and survey photographs of William Henry Jackson (1843-1942), had become by the later nineteenth century the chief vehicle for recording history and communicating about place. Paintings had been relegated to the realm of aesthetics and poetry. There were many reasons for this. The apparently mechanical, unmediated truth of photographs seemed to obviously tell the truth. What Oliver Wendell Holmes called "sun writing" certainly lent an aura of authenticity to these thin, little black and white objects. Also, George Eastman's introduction of the gelatin-coated dry plate in 1880 and the subsequent popularization of flexible film and point-and-shoot box cameras after 1889 put cameras into the hands of the public. As a result, the sheer volume of photographs produced what appeared to be an encyclopedic record of places and communities. Their range accentuated both similarity and difference in the experience of people in all regions, and particularly in the Yellowstone Country.[4]

By the 1880s, the ubiquity of photographed images, particularly portraits, had begun to attract critical comment from writers like Holmes, who wrote: "What the daguerreotype and photograph do is to give the features and one particular look, the very look which kills all expression, that of self-consciousness." There were, of course, exceptions among these photographs and photographers. Some people developed an affinity for the medium: the luck of being at a particularly good place at a particularly good time; an ability to quickly turn an intent eye gazing through the "view-finder" to balance and order an infinity of space within the tiny rectangular frame; a mind which lent itself to the quick calculation necessary to correctly match light conditions, film or plate characteristics, lens aperture, and exposure time. The results of such conditions can be extraordinary images or a body of work produced over a long period by a well-known, little-known or even in many cases anonymous photographer.[5]

Our understanding of photography and place is further complicated by the fact that in Montana (as in much of the Rocky Mountain West and the nation) virtually every town had a professional photographer by the 1880s. They set up shop along with the new churches, schools, bars, pharmacies, and dry-goods and hardware stores. Sometimes initiating their business from tents on a newly scraped and rutted main street, sometimes in their homes, these photographers came to meet what they saw as a social need and a

consumer demand. Like Evelyn Cameron, they sometimes used photography
as a way to supplement their meager income from debt-ridden farms and
ranches. Billings had five major photographers during these years: Laurens,
Gesecus, R.B. Rumsey, Baumgartner, and M.S. Gillette. N.J. Wendt opened
a studio in Boonton; W.H. Culver had a studio first in Lewiston and then in
Maiden (now Maiden Rock, near Helena); the Elite Studio in Butte
produced a number of portraits of African-Americans near the turn of the
century; and Eklund, Christensen, and Benjamin and McIntyre had
businesses in cities like Great Falls, Fort Benton, and Forsyth. They all
portrayed main streets, churches, schools, homes, businesses, ranches, and
people in Montana's young towns.[6]

Not all photographers were professionals. By 1900, there were a large
number of amateur photographers and photography clubs in major towns.
On December 27-31, 1898, for example, the Helena Camera Club hosted an
amateur photography exhibition in the Art Rooms of Wm. Biggs on the
corner of 6th and Jackson streets. Amateur clubs from Missoula, Bozeman,
and Helena and individuals from New York City and Billings exhibited
images ranging from landscape through live game, New England scenery,
genre, and Indians.
Photography businesses
had to establish a place
for themselves in the
midst of a culture which
soon found cameras in
most homes. They did
this by choosing
equipment and using
techniques not readily
available to or
convenient for the
general public.

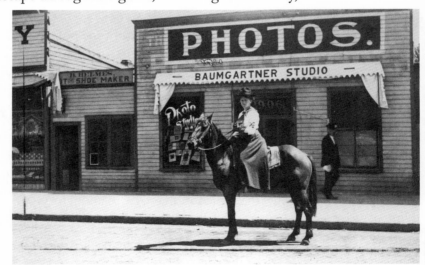

Plate 1

Professionals often favored the large view cameras and the cumbersome wet
and dry plate, collodion processes to produce high quality prints of a
relatively large size. Many tinted and hand-colored their prints, especially

their larger ones, to make their work look more like the "art" of paintings or "chromos," the framed chromolithograph color prints that had earlier been popular as parlor decorations. Evelyn Cameron alluded to this process in a 1926 letter describing her frustration when she had been ". . . two hours tinting the Rainier Print–fearing that I should over tint. In spite of this the shadow ruins the whole endeavor! So I suppose the print will have to be entirely washed tomorrow." Photographers began to think of their prints as framed wall pictures, rather than the hidden rectangles closed in embossed albums.[7]

Professional photographers also specialized. [Plate #1] They specialized in the region with which they were identified and favored particular sorts of views: portraits, commercial interiors, cityscapes, landscapes, Native Americans, hunting scenes, ranch scenes, children, historical events. Baumgartner, in addition to making fashionable portraits of fashionable townspeople, made numerous studio portraits of Crow Indians, including this startling–for its unusual character–portrait of the Baumgartner Family and a group of Crow Indians. [Plate #2] Frank Jay Haynes was identified with Yellowstone National Park scenery. Haynes worked along the line of the railroad, while others turned their gaze away from it. Sometimes in an official capacity as a railroad employee, later as the only authorized "official" photographer of Yellowstone National Park, his audience was the outsider, the visitor, and he showed them what they were coming to see. Laton Alton Huffman, perhaps more than any other photographer of his generation, helped to define the public perception–in practical and mythic terms–of life in the Yellowstone valley. His photographs are full of cowboys, Indians, hunting expeditions, and bison herds. His photographs of the ranches and ranch life of the area around Miles City were a vehicle

Plate 2

through which the citizens of the valley, especially the affluent male citizens, came to understand themselves. And Evelyn Cameron emphasized ranch life as home life and the animals both wild and domesticated of the "Big Open" and the badlands near Terry and Fallon, farther east in the Yellowstone valley. Among these, Cameron was the most introspective, insistently depicting herself and imagining herself within the landscape that the other two looked at more outwardly. She turned her lens toward the domestic lives of the people and animals that inhabited her isolated place in Montana. Her views are intimate, personal, and sometimes uncanny.

What all three photographers shared was the Yellowstone valley of Montana, a very large place in the West. They shared their outsider roots—each came to the state as an adult. And they shared a love for the place from which they parlayed a living of sorts out of the life of the imagination. They were three very different minds creating three authentic but varied representations of this place in the West. And they communicated something of the vastness of the space, and the individuality and character of the people who lived in it, through the small, unassuming, and fragile medium of the photograph.

The Yellowstone River forms the axis of a vast basin of eastern Montana that in the last third of the nineteenth century became a distinguishable, separate "place in the West." It was along the axis formed by the river that settlement took place. The river also formed the main route of transportation across the territory and the backbone for its agricultural development. Its bottomlands offered both watered fields and the possibility of wider irrigation in the midst of the northern portion of what the explorers like Captain Stephen Long had called in 1820 the "Great American Desert" west of the hundredth meridian.[8]

Settlement followed this route during the 1870s and 1880s. The expansion of the culture of eastern North America into the unconsolidated territories west of the hundredth meridian after the Civil War moved into the territory from both the east and the west. Fort Union lay at the eastern end of the valley, at the river's mouth on the Missouri. A painter, George Catlin, travelled there in 1832 on the *Yellowstone*, the first steam-powered vessel to ascend this far up the Missouri River to paint what he called the "disappearing races" of the Plains Indians—especially Crow and Blackfeet. It was a thriving trading fort, established years after Lewis and Clark first explored the region in the name of the youthful United States nearly three decades earlier. By the 1870s, this route along the Yellowstone River was the surveyed line along which the Northern Pacific would complete the third transcontinental railroad, between St. Paul and Tacoma in 1883.[9]

Six hundred miles away, at the other end of the river, lay its headwaters on the high plateau south of Yellowstone National Park. This area of thermal fantasy and extravagant scenery was first brought to the widespread attention of eastern North America in a series of articles by Nathaniel Langford in *Scribner's Magazine* in 1872. As with most reports of the West after the Civil War, the public demanded visual corroboration for the fantastic narratives of the explorers, so the article was illustrated with wood engravings by a then little-known artist named Thomas Moran. Although he was to establish a national reputation on the basis of his monumental painting of the Grand Canyon of the Yellowstone of 1872, Moran completed his illustrations for the Langford article without the benefit of ever having seen what he was depicting. In 1872, he and the photographer William Henry Jackson had accompanied the Hayden expedition and the combined work of the painter and the photographer were instrumental in convincing Congress to protect the upper Yellowstone as a national park. The route that Moran took to join the expedition circled south, taking him on the Union Pacific Railroad along the route of the old Oregon Trail into Utah. From there he travelled north by stagecoach through Idaho and Montana into Yellowstone Country.[10]

My point is two-fold. First, the history of the Yellowstone River and the scenery of region it defines are framed at both ends by images which established the region and its boundaries in the minds of easterners, some who would come and others who would never make the trip. Far more powerfully than phrases like the great American Desert, Great Northern Plains, the Rocky Mountains, or even Yellowstone National Park ever could, pictures by painters like Catlin and Moran fixed in easterners' imaginations what was the defining character of this place in the West: the high plains and badlands of the eastern end of the Yellowstone River Valley and the volcanic mountains at the river's source. Second, the Yellowstone River Valley became known—and was settled—from both ends to the middle. It was the region of central Montana between what is now Livingston and Glendive that was the last settled and, for outsiders and Montanans alike, the least known, the least imaginatively defined. This definition largely took place in the years between the inexorable progress of the Northern Pacific across the Northern Plains during the early 1880s and the crushing Great Depression which changed Montana along with the rest of North America, pressing it, sometimes painfully, into a new era. The vehicles that made the area a specific and identifiable place was, largely, pictures: paintings and, even more, photographs. The new residents of the territory used these images to define themselves and communicate that definition to outsiders.

Frank Jay Haynes is perhaps the most widely recognized photographer of the northern Rocky Mountains. He was certainly not the first, but through luck, persistence, and extremely acute business sense, he realized the photographic and financial possibilities opened by the railroad into the Yellowstone valley. He attached himself to the transportation business and attached the technology of photography to the railroad by literally hitching his wagon to the train. He created images calculated to attract settlers to the newly opened farmland of the high, dry plains to attract business investments to new and thriving commercial centers like Billings and Miles City, and to attract tourists to the spectacular scenery and "frontier" character of the Yellowstone valley. And these attractive images of his were all in the service of the promotional interests of the Northern Pacific Railroad.

Haynes was born on October 28, 1853, in Saline, Michigan, and worked at his father's store there until it failed in 1874. In his early twenties began to dabble in photography. For two years he worked in the studio of S.C. Graham in Beaver Dam, Wisconsin, and then in William H. Lockwood's New Temple of Photographic Art in Ripon. There he met—and later married—Lily Verna Snyder, Lockwood's sister-in-law. And there, in April 1876, he first experienced the advantages of silver paper and print negatives in a portable studio—Lockwood's excursion boat, the *Camera*.[11]

By fall of 1876, he joined his sister Ella Henderson, who had moved to Moorehead, Minnesota, with her merchant husband, and "was urging him to come West where photographers were scarce."[12]

The move was fortuitous. Shortly after his coming to Moorehead, the Northern Pacific, which used the city as its jumping-off point into the Northern Plains, commissioned him to illustrate its appeals to settlers to migrate along its routes. Some years later he illustrated a brochure published by the Great Northern Railway that proclaimed, "Photographs Tell the Truth" followed by the pitch:

> These pictures are selected and published for the Benefit of People who are interested in the Great Northwest. They are reproductions of photographs, and are therefore absolutely truthful. They give, in a very pleasing way, a perfect picture of the homes and farms of the most attractive part of Uncle Sam's Big Farm.[13]

All photographs were "on the line of the Northern Pacific Railway."

By 1878 Haynes had married Lily Snyder and moved his studio to Fargo, across the Red River in the Dakota Territory on the Northern Pacific's line. L.A. Huffman worked briefly in his studio, before setting off in 1878 for Fort Keogh on the Yellowstone, beyond the reach of the railroad. Very quickly Haynes began making trips on the Northern Pacific lines to record the "Bonanza Farms" along the Red River Valley.

Haynes made his first trip to the new Yellowstone National Park in 1881, travelling by stage from Glendive to Livingston and south into the park. Glendive, not far from the Old Fort Union, was the end of the track that spring, and Livingston was planned as the departure point for a Northern Pacific spur to the Yellowstone National Park. Haynes agreed with the Northern Pacific developers and with Philetus Norris, the first superintendent of the park who claimed, "The scenery is superior to the Yosemite Valley of California," and on July 18, 1881, had filed his application to the become the official Yellowstone National Park Photographer. He photographed throughout the park for the next few summers as well as along the Northern Pacific line. In the summer of 1883 he served as guide for President Chester Arthur, and the following year visited the park with M.L. Joslyn, the secretary of the interior, who allowed Haynes a ten-year lease for a shop at the Upper Geyser Basin.[14]

Also in 1883 Haynes recorded the procession of the Frederick Billings and Henry Villard Excursion along the Northern Pacific line, recording ceremonies, depots, pageants, and speeches all the way to Helena, where on September 13, 1883, a newspaper proclaimed:

> A dream no longer! This fateful day Brings the east and the west
> alike; The closing act in the wondrous play Is–driving the
> Golden Spike![15]

He continued to work for the railroad, becoming its official photographer in 1883. By 1885 he had adapted a railroad coach as the "Haynes Palace Studio Car," which operated under his direction making photography stops in towns with depots along the length of the Northern Pacific's route in the Dakota and Montana territories. He always combined both his own business interests with promoting the park and the surrounding countryside of the Yellowstone valley–including an 1877 image of the Custer Battlefield, an 1885 image of a "Petrified Indian"–and selling retail photographs, often mounted against "pine cone paper" backgrounds, to private parties and the Department of the Interior.[16]

In 1889 he moved his studio from Fargo to St. Paul. Haynes produced an enormous volume of images, but by far the largest number of subjects came from Yellowstone National Park. He produced these images in a vast array of types, ranging from simple, mass-printed post cards the most expensive platinum prints and hand-tinted, or crayon-touched, framed images. Of these, one of his most frequent subjects was Mammoth Hot Springs, the first large thermal area in the park that the tourist would see after arriving at Gardiner, Montana, on the Northern Pacific spur. Of these, an often repeated subject was Minerva Terrace [Plate #3]–of which W.H. Jackson had made several images ten years before, including a famous one

Plate 3

102

which posed the painter Thomas Moran on the travertine terraces. Like many of his large framed prints, this one (dating from about 1900) was hand painted and panoramic in format: narrow from top to bottom and extremely wide, more than twice as wide as high. Like the luminist landscapes that were in fashion during the previous quarter century, this photograph emphasized transparent contrasts of light and dark in an insistently horizontal format of bands and light and dark.[17] Haynes framed the terraces of the hot spring tightly so that it filled the already large rectangle and seemed to expand off the left and right edges of the frame. The image emphasized both the size of the "mammoth" spring and through its close attention to texture and insistent exclusion of anything human to give it scale, the wildness, even weirdness of the scene, which the Northern Pacific would catalogue in its advertisement of its territory:

> To the Land Explorer, To the Business Man, To the Farmer, To the Mechanic, To the Laborer, To the Sportsman, To the Tourist, To the Miner, To All Classes, For the Raising of Wheat, For the Raising of Stock, For Ready and Cash Markets, For a Healthy Climate, For Sure and Good Crops, For Remunerative Investments, For Business Opportunities, For Weird Scenery, The Northern Pacific Country Has No Equal.[18]

Significantly, Frank Jay Haynes and L.A. Huffman, the two most well-known photographers of the Yellowstone valley, each of whom came to be securely associated with his own corner of Montana, briefly worked together before ever coming to the Yellowstone valley from the Midwest. Huffman, himself the son of a professional photographer in Iowa, worked for Haynes in his studio in the Dakota Territory in 1878. From there he moved to the wide-open territory of the opening Northern Plains, taking the job as the post photographer at Fort Keogh, which had been built on the frontier during the staging of the Plains Indian Wars in the 1870s, near what would become Miles City, Montana. Huffman arrived just two years after the Battle of the Little Big Horn, the last great victory of the Native American resistance on the Northern Plains. He arrived in the decade in which the Plains nations were conclusively located on reservations, the buffalo herds were almost completely annihilated, and the railroads were confirming their hold on the transcontinental routes across the western part of the continent.

He wasn't the first photographer in this part of the West, nor even the first photographer at Fort Keogh—a base photographer preceded him there several years.[19]

Upon the photographer's dismissal, Huffman replaced him and worked at Keogh briefly until opening a permanent log studio in Miles City, across the Yellowstone. His long life and career spanned the time from early ranching days on the open range through the arrival of the railroad construction crews moving up the Yellowstone valley out of North Dakota and the coming of barbed wire and smaller farms and real towns. He also witnessed the settlement that followed hard on the heels of the Native Americans, as they were removed to reservations in south of the Yellowstone River at what is now the Crow reservation, into the Dakotas, and north of the Missouri River in Montana. As soon as the migrations stopped, the settlers came, brought in endless numbers by the iron horse. Because of the relative lateness of the settlement of the high plains east of the Rocky Mountains, a constellation of images of the West was already firmly fixed in the eastern public's mind. Many of the settlers who came to these high, dry plains succeeded only by reconciling the image they had brought with them with the people and geography they found there. Huffman played a significant role in that reconciliation.

Much like Catlin forty years before in the same region (if slightly farther east), Huffman created an enormous body of work attempting to retrieve lost time. He recorded for the imagination things that were perceived to be disappearing, trying to make visible and permanent what was helplessly fading from view, and celebrating, as it were, the charm of extinction. His subjects: the bison herds that the onslaught of the railroad and the hunter diminished; the Indian nations that were falling to disease and impoundment; the open range that was being divided up by settlers even as Huffman photographed it. Even the two books celebrating his accomplishment—*The Frontier Years* and *Before Barbed Wire*—suggest something of the ways in which his photographs are still in the late twentieth century perceived to be the last record of a disappearing way of life. One of the hallmarks of his work is his fascination with Native American burials—sandstone caves, tree burials, burial platforms, and even, as in one photograph, a wagon on wheels impressed into the service of the dead.

The techniques that Huffman used in the adaptations of photographs from the album to the wall [Plate #4] are evident in his attempt to monumentalize and make beautiful the sheer, stark space of the plains and the deadpan accuracy of the photographic prints he

Plate 4

made. Here are the facts: a few buffalo standing on the desiccated grass of the rangeland north of Miles City. With the exception of a single buffalo scene, the entire collection of framed Huffman photos in the collection is hand-tinted, and even with the spare use of watercolor and gouache in these images, it seems clear that a twentieth-century taste for sepia and the severities of black and white was not shared by Huffman, Cameron, or Haynes. Huffman used color here variously to allude to the color of paintings and to make these pictures do things that the technology of photography simply couldn't do in creating an image of the Montana plains in the years around the turn of the century.

Here, as in many of the pictures, his horizontal format of the composition is emphasized by broad bands in which he paints the ground in an even tone of gold, the sky in uniform, cloudless blue. The gold of the plains is punctuated with small, variegated areas of green, particularly around touched-in, calligraphic references to bunchgrass and grama. The sky is a broad, lightly varied wash of watercolor blue, reticulated on the right where the watercolor unevenly caught the grain of the paper, effectively creating the impression of an atmospheric sky. Along the horizon is a half-inch area where the color overlaps the golden tones of the lands creating a deepening of color where the sky meets the land. This area is further touched in with blue and taupe and lavender. The effect is one of pearly light and richly varied color at odds with the typical black and white surfaces of photographic negatives. The coloring emphasizes the horizon, which would otherwise be a much fainter grey, nearly indistinguishable from sky and earth.

Huffman frames the bison in front of a low rise of land at a point in the otherwise unbroken horizon almost directly in the center of the image. The hand-coloring further clarifies the bison showing in the paint, as in the case of the big guy in the middle, the rough texture of his coat. But the animals further back, especially on the left behind what appears to be a low ridge, appear as virtually undistinguishable darker gray masses. The effect is

that Huffman carefully picks out the "subject" of his photograph, virtually by painting it in. The result is a public image, by no means simply a straightforward record which by emphasis and suppression recreate the myth of eastern Montana that was rapidly passing

Plate 5

into history. The story that he insistently tells of Miles City and the surrounding countryside is precisely that story which he perceives to be coming to an end. The buffalo are disappearing, the range is getting fenced— and the Big Open is coming to a close.

Like virtually all of Evelyn Cameron's prints from glass plate photographs, "Evelyn and the Williams sisters on Dolly" [Plate #5], looks squarely at its subject in the middle of the frame. Against a bare horizon, the photographer sits between her friends, Janet and Mabel Williams, on the reluctant horse who kept "turning her head to eye the three passengers."[20] Behind the riders two hills slope down to the horse from either side, fixing them before the whitened fence posts that mark space and time across the undifferentiated grass prairie. The horse squints. The women smile, Evelyn broadly. The whole picture was itself a sign, a kind of billboard, like the sign that it contained advertising "Photos by E. Cameron, Fallon, Mont." The photograph was also a sign of other things, some past, some to come. This photographer emphasized here, as she frequently did, her place in a larger place: an Englishwoman on the high dry grassland of the Yellowstone valley in eastern Montana. The photograph shows something of the importance of friendship in a lonely land that sometimes looks empty even to those who love it. In order to record the minute characteristics of the faces, Cameron needed to expose her glass plate slowly. The light coming from above and to the right picks out the fine detail of facet and plane in the women's faces and the texture of their clothing, but the grass moves in the foreground and blurs into the distance; the sky is white and void, so full of light that the crystalline emulsion on the glass plate bleaches out the texture of atmosphere and weather into a space that is void above the horizon. This effect exaggerates the line separating earth and sky, as though the empty plain rolls back to an to an oddly close, opaque blank wall. The effect echoes the photography of Cameron's earlier contemporary, Laton Alton Huffman, in his images of the area surrounding Miles City. There is little here, as in those earlier images, to mark the distance to the stark horizon, but a great deal to mark the emptiness, and the isolation of the figures in the near center of the space.

In Cameron's photograph advertising herself, the women float in this space. The more one looks at the image, the more it becomes almost surreal— these three figures arranged like a chorus line above the horizon. The sign, the same shape and size as the glass photographic plate itself, seems to be almost tacked onto the front of the image instead of hanging precariously on Dolly's neck. Four feet hang below the three women. Rather than the more proper side-saddle, one, maybe two, of the women are riding astride in split skirts, a style which the photographer herself introduced to the Montana plains. She wore them with some degree of defiance and at some risk herself. Early in her residency, she risked arrest for wearing such clothes into Miles City. But these women are not in the town; they are, except for the camera, apparently alone in the space.[21]

What is this place? What does the photograph show? What does it mean? Among other things, it suggests, at the very least, that this place is in the West—the rural West of the plains ranchland—treeless, trackless, and wide open. Cameron shows us this in the breadth of the landscape that surrounds and frames the three women hovering on the horse. She also shows us something of the social character of her photography. The women sit upright, the photographer framed by the two Williams sisters, who are among her best friends.[22]

Donna Lucey characterizes the picture as one "which Evelyn used to advertise her photography business in 1910."[23] As with the Baumgartner advertisement [Plate #1], the point consists of a horsewoman and sign imagined squarely on home turf, viewed straight on: photographs by and of *this* people, in *this* place. We are judging Cameron, of course, by a contemporary print from the original glass plate. Somehow Cameron had printed and circulated the image, or so it appears. We don't really know much about the prints that she made, in what quantities she made them, or how widely they advertised her business. Only the original exposure appears to have survived, declaring with dead-on directness both that the range near Terry and Fallon in Prairie County is a place, and that place was only to be understood as belonging to her and to her community of friends and customers. In her imagination, and on her glass plates, Cameron created the place, framing it carefully, and repeatedly, unabashedly locating herself squarely at its heart. We can't really understand her without these images of place. Nor can we understand the place that she created apart from her self and her imagination.

That's essentially the lesson that the photographers of the Yellowstone valley have to teach. What we know about this place—about any place, even "the West"—a couple of generations ago is inevitably through particular eyes, realized through particular imaginations. It's their ability to invoke the particular and the individual that imparts to photographs their force. Here that force is imaginatively condensed into visions at once institutional, communal, and domestic. In photographs this imaginative power is the power to give to Montana an image that is spatial, rather than narrative.

Rather than telling stories, each photographer has created a personal place, whether private or public, in a way similar to the aims of a book like *Montana Spaces* images refract and inflect an infinity of possibilities into images, crystalline in every way, of the ordinariness and the peculiarity of individual place [Plate A in photographic section following page 92], spatial, patterned, ordered around private perspective and a shifting, public imagination.[24]

"And I was used to goin' to church and to Sunday School and everything. And out here in the God–forsaken country, no churches, no, nobody even mentioned church. You never heard the bible read, you never heard nobody sain' a prayer or nothin', and I, I just, I thought I was livin' in a regular heathen country." Lillian Stephenson

"Her and I lived in the sheepwagon. We did. She tended camp and I herded, and we made it. Prices come up a little, and we weren't out no expense of herders or anything. And then the next thing, by God here, Jimmy was born. So we had to change again. And come and live here instead of the sheepwagon." Red Killen

"Really that was the most because everybody during the drought deals in the '30s and whatnot they headed for the coast and the war situation was on here and the ships made a lot of work. So a big share of those people went to the coast, California. . . . They would just have the old train loaded with people. And they couldn't hardly keep them all off because when the train got out of the yard, why it was moving, and if it slowed down like going over the mountain here, the people on the mountain would climb on the train and on their way they went. They couldn't hardly stop them." Lester Gilbert

"Well, there must have been drought, too, because I remember Dad and Uncle Whit moved their cattle over north, and I can remember helping them bring them back. That must have been around '20 or '21. . . ."

There were four, five of us, I remember. I should say four and a kid. But we got 'em all gathered up and start across, but we didn't have anybody in the lead like we should of had. The cattle started trotting, and boy, that old bridge just swayed like that. And of course without anybody in the lead, when they got over to the other side, they just scattered. Everybody's yard. Course there weren't many yards over there like there is now, which is a good thing. I can remember the cattle running under one clothesline and a woman out there swinging an apron at them."
Whit Longley

"No matter where they went, it was tough. It was bad every place. The whole United States, Canada was all bad. As I told ya', one time we had a garden by the railroad track near the ditch there. And that, that particular day I counted the men sitting on the boxcars and flatcars. And there were sixty men I counted on their way to Sidney lookin' for work. That afternoon, there would be that many goin' back. Next day that many goin' again. Just work, nothin'. No work, no money. No nothing. Hire the best of men for a dollar a day. And boy, they would work, too. You just go to town to get a, pick up a hired man, and you just, in the pool halls and stuff, you just about feel of everybody's arm. If you didn't have a big strong arm, you didn't bother about him. . . . A lot of them were educated, too. Pitiful part, sometimes you'd see a man and a wife and a little baby or two goin' down the road carryin' a little kid. And they would stop in your garden, and dig up a hill or two of potatoes, and pull a few carrots—we had a garden near the railroad track—and they would eat that. They never destroyed anything. And then, they didn't steal off ya'." August Sobotka

good times, bad times: the economic transformation of the yellowstone valley, 1880-1940

carroll van west

In 1880, census takers who visited the Yellowstone valley counted only 588 people living in the vast area between present-day Livingston and Miles City. Far fewer residents lived in the rangeland east of Miles City. Such current urban landmarks as Billings, Livingston, and Glendive did not even exist. Over the next two generations, however, corporate investors, aggressive civic capitalists, hopeful homesteaders, and committed urban pioneers took advantage of the Yellowstone's geographical location, its natural resources, and recent changes in federal land policies to create a landscape of irrigated fields, modern transportation systems, coal mines, urban centers, and sugar beet factories that only the most ambitious boosters of 1880 could have imagined.

The integration of the Yellowstone valley into the national railroad network was the first step toward transforming this rural countryside into a modern settlement landscape. In 1879, the Northern Pacific Railroad emerged from bankruptcy and renewed its drive westward from the banks of the Missouri River at Bismarck. Company officials, led by its president Frederick Billings, aimed the tracks straight for the heart of the Yellowstone valley. "If we go by the Yellowstone it will be a long time before anybody gets to the north of us," Billings remarked to Thomas Doane in late 1879. "Besides the Big Horn Country and that region are full of mineral deposits and you may consider the Yellowstone as the route." The untapped resources of the valley would maximize the potential riches contained in the railroad's generous land grant–an eighty-mile-wide path with alternating sections belonging to the company. The land grant was always the Northern Pacific's best asset, and company officials believed that more investors would be attracted to company stock if the tracks ran along the Yellowstone.[1]

The Northern Pacific entered the Yellowstone valley during the summer of 1881. At the point where the railroad first crossed the Yellowstone River, a group of past and present Northern Pacific officials and investors—led by Major Lewis Merrill, Henry Douglas, J. W. Raymond, and J. W. Kendrick—incorporated themselves as the Yellowstone Land and Colonization Company and established Glendive. Armed with advance notice of the railroad's plans to establish a division point at its first Yellowstone crossing, the land company grabbed most of the land on the east bank of the river and platted a symmetrically designed grid town, which replaced the frontier settlement that had stood on the mesa south of Glendive Creek. Douglas, the Northern Pacific's commissary agent, built the town's first store. Together with his brother-in-law David R. Mead, he soon established the Douglas & Mead Mercantile Company, a business that continued to operate until 1954. Douglas also owned the local ferry service, a lumberyard, the HS Cattle Company, and Merchants' National Bank. To further secure his company's investments, Douglas offered the railroad free bricks to build its extensive machine shops at Glendive. The Northern Pacific readily accepted, forever linking the town's fortunes to those of the railroad.[2]

What happened at Glendive in the summer of 1881 would be repeated as the Northern Pacific moved swiftly past Miles City, reaching Billings in the summer of 1882 and Livingston during the last month of that year. Livingston and Billings were planned on grids strictly oriented to the tracks. The railroad bypassed previously existing settlements to establish the new towns. Company officials and investors used insider information to grab the best land and create land companies that would hold a monopoly on the urban development of the valley. Both cities served as mainline division points; indeed, Livingston quickly emerged as one of the company's most important regional bases. By 1883, its two thousand residents made Livingston the largest town in the valley. Compared to the other towns, Livingston had two immediate advantages: it served as the "Gateway" to Yellowstone National Park, and its machine shops were the company's largest between the West Coast and the eastern terminus at Brainerd, Minnesota.[3]

Livingston's preeminent position in the railroad network of the Yellowstone valley stood unchallenged for the first decade of settlement. Once the Northern Pacific emerged from bankruptcy after the depression of 1893-1896, Livingston experienced a second railroad-induced boom when the company greatly expanded its machine shops in about 1900 and built a grand Italian Renaissance-styled depot to serve as its official Yellowstone gateway. The town's population almost doubled between 1900 and 1904 and then increased another 55 percent during the next five years. By 1909 the Northern Pacific employed 1,178 at its extensive works, making Livingston the railroad's most important stop in the Yellowstone valley.[4]

By this time, however, Livingston was no longer the most important transportation center in the Yellowstone valley. Due to luck, international corporate maneuvering, and its geographical location, Billings and the neighboring town of Laurel emerged between 1894 and 1908 as a rail center for the entire Northern Plains. This transportation infrastructure, in turn, provided part of the foundation for the rather amazing economic expansion of Billings and Yellowstone County in the early twentieth century, turning what had been a place of grandiose ambitions but little potential into the urban heart of the Yellowstone valley.[5] In 1894, a branch line of the Chicago, Burlington, and Quincy (popularly known as the Burlington Route) entered the Yellowstone valley, joining the Northern Pacific at Billings. The two companies already signed an agreement that opened Burlington's tracks east of Billings to eastbound Northern Pacific trains, while westbound Burlington traffic could use Northern Pacific rails west of Billings. As soon as the first Burlington train reached Billings in October 1894, the town immediately became a signficant railroad center, linking Burlington's midwestern urban markets to the natural resources of the Northwest. Its success led Burlington executives to plan their own northwest extension to the Pacific Coast. As company president Charles E. Perkins remarked in May 1895: "With our Montana line in operation to Billings, we are in so strong a position for offense that I feel quite comfortable about it."[6] The activities of the Northern Pacific and the Burlington during 1893-1894 caught the wary eye of James J. Hill, the St. Paul railroad magnate who just a few years earlier had completed his own transcontinental rail link, the Great Northern Railway, from St. Paul to the Pacific Northwest. The Burlington extension had been pointed at Billings since 1889, when Hill realized the threat it posed to his own plans for the region. Perhaps not by coincidence, Hill made his first efforts to gain control of the Northern Pacific in 1889, and when that proved impossible he quickly finished his main line from Havre, Montana, to the West Coast.[7]

After the depression of 1893 forced the Northern Pacific into bankruptcy, Hill renewed his efforts to acquire his major Montana competitor. But powerful financiers like August Belmont and, ultimately, J. Pierpont Morgan opposed his move for absolute control over the Northern Pacific. Morgan wanted the railroad's reorganization to be part of a general restructuring of western railroad transportation. Nonetheless, Hill temporarily gained the upper hand in 1894 when the Northern Pacific's considerable number of German investors, represented by the Deutsche Bank of Berlin, asked him and his partner Lord Mount Stephen, the former Canadian Pacific Railroad president, for assistance in reorganizing the railroad. A group of American investors, who had been linked to former Northern Pacific president Frederick Billings, also asked Hill and Stephen to come to the rescue. Excited by the prospect, Hill wrote his New York banker that taking control of the Northern Pacific was "beyond doubt a very desirable thing to do."[8]

Hill lost his advantage in the spring of 1895, when his own reorganization plan gained little support. That April, Stephen met with J. P.

Morgan and Dr. George Siemens of the Deutsche Bank to hammer out a compromise solution. In early May, Hill and representatives of the Northern Pacific signed a memorandum of agreement known as the "London Agreement," which called for the Great Northern to guarantee payment on the principal and interest of a newly reorganized Northern Pacific in exchange for half of the Northern Pacific's stock; joint use of certain selected tracks and depots; and friendly relations in all traffic matters. Due to political pressure, public opinion, and questions about its legality under Minnesota state law, the agreement soon fell apart. Officials of the Burlington Route briefly considered taking advantage of the situation by acquiring the Northern Pacific itself; but after board chairman John M. Forbes warned that Burlington would have to kill James J. Hill first to grab the Northern Pacific, company officials backed away, deciding that it was actually in the Burlington's interest for the Great Northern to control the Northern Pacific.[9]

During the next four years, the Great Northern gained control of the Northern Pacific, with banker J. P. Morgan in charge of the reorganization. In April 1896, Morgan, Hill, Stephen, and Arthur Gwinner, a director of the Deutsche Bank, signed the "London memorandum," which stipulated that the Great Northern and the Northern Pacific would establish "a permanent alliance" that would minimize competition and protect their common interests. Although Hill and Morgan repeatedly clashed about its exact meaning, the new agreement gave Hill indirect control over almost all rail transportation in the Northern Plains. He consolidated his power in late 1900 when Morgan dissolved his voting trust that had directed Northern Pacific operations, leaving the Great Northern in charge of the line. Morgan then financed Hill's acquisition of a controlling interest in the Chicago, Burlington, and Quincy. To secure his control over Northern Pacific affairs, Hill would also greatly increase the amount of NP stock he privately owned, from about $1.5 million in January 1901 to almost $10 million five years later. Hill later bragged that this intense period of financial wrangling and corporate maneuvering "paved the way for the new era" in western transportation.[10]

The corporate restructuring certainly introduced a "new era" for the towns along the Northern Pacific mainline in the Yellowstone valley. Infused with a new injection of investment capital, the Northern Pacific expanded lines and its machine shops, especially at Livingston. But the biggest dividends were reserved for Billings, where two of the three lines in Hill's nascent railroad empire already met. In the fall of 1900, Great Northern officials announced that the "Great Falls and Billings Railway," would soon link the two transcontinentals with the Burlington at Billings. The *Billings Gazette* confidently predicted that the new connection "would soon make Billings the trade center of eastern and central Montana." But another round of corporate warfare over the control of the Northern Pacific, this time between Hill and Edward Harriman of the Union Pacific and Southern Pacific railroads, delayed Hill's plans for a central railroad transfer point in Yellowstone County. Not until 1905 would the legal and financial fallout from this struggle of railroad titans be resolved. It concluded largely in Hill's favor, and his control over the Great Northern, Northern Pacific, and Burlington never again faced a serious challenge. In 1906, Hill looked at the Billings yards and decided that insufficient space existed for the traffic interchange point for the three lines. He moved the new joint yards to the nearby village of Laurel, where there was plenty of room for growth and expansion. Billings boomed as had no other town in the history of the Yellowstone valley. Whereas the city directory placed the city's population at near 7,000 in 1906, the following year it estimated that Billings had reached between 12,000 and 13,000 residents.[11]

The corporate realignment of the northwestern railroad network set the stage for a remarkable boom in Billings and Yellowstone County between 1905 and 1915. The city became a prominent point on American railroad maps. But railroads and high finance alone do not account for the economic transformation and resurgence of Billings in the early twentieth century. Geographer John Hudson has recently observed that "railroads simply did not bring about urbanization"; more typically they created "chains of small trade centers, not chains of great cities." So we should look elsewhere for other key contributors to the development of Billings and Yellowstone County in the early twentieth century. The presence of aggressive local civic and commercial leaders, who banded together to work for their mutually shared interests, proved especially important. A 1907 history of the city admitted that Billings enjoyed a "strategic position in Northwestern commerce" that made it "the natural gateway to the entire northwest." But "admirable location" and "splendid railway service" meant little compared "to the enterprise and public spirit of its business men." Historian John Cumbler has defined these local entrepreneurs as "civic capitalists," who sought their "own profit, but each understood that his welfare was bound up with the welfare of others of his kind and the city that nourished them."[12]

The tradition of civic capitalism began early in Billings' history and centered on the activities of the Frederick Billings family. A former president of the Northern Pacific, Frederick Billings had been one of the original owners of the Minnesota and Montana Land and Improvement Company, which possessed almost 30,000 acres in the Yellowstone valley, where it developed the town of Billings. As the settlement grew between 1882 and 1884, Billings and his wife Julia donated money for the first church and school, and throughout the late 1880s, he willingly invested in projects, ranging from artesian wells in Billings to the coal mines at Red Lodge to the coke ovens and smelter plant at Livingston.[13]

He reserved his most personal investments, however, for the town of Billings and Yellowstone County. By 1884, he owned more than 4,500 acres in and about Billings before acquiring absolute control of the land company that spring. Dissatisfied with the local managerial talent available in Billings, he sent his son Parmly and his nephew Edward Bailey to manage the family property. The younger Billings and Bailey joined all of the important local commercial and social clubs–Parmly was even approached to run for mayor– and they established an important engine of capital in their Billings and Bailey private bank. Even after Parmly's unexpected death in 1888 and the passing of his father two years later, the Billings family remained interested in business affairs in Billings through its continued supervision of the land company's operations.[14]

But the removal of the family's direct personal involvement opened doors for new class of entrepreneurs to make their mark on Billings during the 1890s. Albert L. Babcock, a native of New York, was the first to step forward. In partnership with A. W. Miles, he had opened one of the town's first hardware stores in 1882. Nine years later, he purchased control of the former Billings and Bailey Bank and established the Yellowstone National Bank, where he served as president from 1893 to his death in 1918. A year after the Burlington extension arrived in 1894, he used his financial clout to open several important businesses, including the Yellowstone Valley Flouring Mill, the Billings Opera House, and the Billings Telephone Company. His economic power also translated into political power. Babcock was a leader of the local Republican party and served as state senator from 1894 to 1898.[15]

Preston B. Moss was another local banker to emerge as a future economic leader in the Yellowstone valley. A native of Missouri, Moss moved to Billings in 1892 to be the vice-president of the First National Bank. Four years later he became the bank's president and invested in new Billings enterprises and Yellowstone County agricultural projects. He also owned a local telephone company, the Northern Hotel, the Gazette Printing Company, and the Billings Utility Company.[16]

His most important investments, however, came in tandem with I.D. O'Donnell, a former cowboy at the Billings family ranch who served as the on-site manager of the Minnesota and Montana Land and Improvement Company. O'Donnell occupied a special place in the early twentieth century history of Billings and Yellowstone County. He was a link to the region's frontier beginnings—indeed he became the first serious chronicler of that history—as well as its early dependence on the Billings family. In about 1890, he purchased the former landholdings of Parmly Billings, creating the partnership of Bailey and O'Donnell. "We fed a number of bands of sheep, took up various land holdings and kept a quantity of range," O'Donnell later recalled. "It was through these experiments that I caught a glimpse of a great future for farming in the Yellowstone Valley." During the 1890s, he began to develop a national reputation as an expert in irrigation and learned to experiment with new agricultural crops like alfalfa and sugar beets. In 1898, he even received a patent for a new irrigation headgate design. The new century would find O'Donnell leading the effort to acquire federal water projects and sugar beet factories for the Yellowstone valley. He proved to be a model "civic capitalist," investing not only in local agriculture and industry but in local banks (a director of the Merchants National Bank) and almost every civic position imaginable, from president of the Midland Empire Fair to the public school board to president of Billings Polytechnic Institute, the first school of higher education in the central valley. A December 1913 editorial in the *Billings Gazette* bragged:

> In Billings, there are many men, who are really doing things, who have the right mental attitude. They make up the predominating influence of society, they lead, and the result is that the right mental attitude, the spirit, the loyalty of the Billings citizen has become provincial throughout the land.

In the newspaper's opinion, O'Donnell was the "Doctor of Mental Attitude" in the Yellowstone valley.[17]

I.D. O'Donnell brought agricultural expertise, innovative ideas, limitless energy, and useful connections to the Yellowstone valley, but Preston Moss brought the most necessary ingredient–investment capital. O'Donnell and Moss combined in their first major venture in October 1900 by purchasing the remaining landholdings of the Minnesota and Montana Land and Improvement Company in October 1900. They turned several sections into the Suburban Homes Company, which sold five-acre urban farmsteads as well as larger tracts. O'Donnell served as the project's secretary and gave promotional lectures wherever he could on the value of irrigated lands and the potential of new crops like sugar beets. Having grown the valley's first sugar beets in 1898, he realized that outsiders were looking with interest at the agricultural potential of the Billings area. In April 1900, an agricultural expert told O'Donnell: "The time is surely coming when Montana will produce its own sugar. You have all the conditions down there to make such a plant a success."[18]

O'Donnell and Moss had great interest in establishing a sugar beet refinery in Billings, but the scattered holdings of the old land company could not provide enough farm acreage. To acquire the needed land at the lowest possible cost, O'Donnell and Moss turned to recent federal laws designed to encourage the irrigation of the arid West. In 1903, a group of Washington state investors came to Billings to investigate the possibility of establishing an irrigation project on the Billings Bench northeast of the city. They wanted to take advantage of the Carey Act of 1894, which granted free federal land to states for major irrigation projects. After touring the capitalists across town and around the county, O'Donnell convinced them that Yellowstone County was indeed the right place to invest. In late October 1903, John Schram and W.T. Clark of Washington and P.B. Moss, I.D. O'Donnell, and Henry Rowley of Billings incorporated the Billings Land & Irrigation Company. A former engineer for the Minnesota and Montana Land and

Improvement Company, Rowley was a neighbor and frequent investor in the schemes hatched by Moss and O'Donnell. The Washington investors put up $75,000, which was matched by $50,000 from Moss and his First National Bank and $12,500 apiece from local businessmen M.A. Arnold and Henry W. Rowley. By 1905, the construction of the irrigation system was largely complete, cultivation was underway, and in April the company received its first land deeds from state officials who administered the Carey Land Act board. The project ultimately irrigated some 24,000 acres.[19]

By 1905, Moss and O'Donnell had also taken advantage of the most recent federal irrigation law, the Newlands Reclamation Act of 1902, which provided federal funding and support for large-scale irrigation projects. O'Donnell knew of a perfect place for such a project: the 35,000 acres around the small rural village of Huntley. The land still belonged to the Crow Indians, but that proved to be only a minor obstacle to businessmen with political connections. In 1904, the federal government negotiated a new Crow land cession, acquiring lands south of the Yellowstone River and along the Big Horn River valley. Federal surveys began in April 1904 and a year later, on April 18, 1905, the secretary of interior approved the "Huntley Irrigation Project"; construction of the primary irrigation ditch began immediately. By that September, the U.S. Reclamation Service had established its northwest headquarters at Billings.[20] On March 14, 1905, Moss, O'Donnell, and Rowley launched their biggest venture yet by incorporating the Billings Sugar Company. Moss bankrolled most of the company by putting up $650,000, while O'Donnell and Rowley each invested $25,000, as did two other Billings businessmen named M.A. Arnold and F.M. Shaw. Two months later, the company signed a contract with the Great Western Sugar Company to provide sugar refined from sugar beets. Billings now had its first truly large locally owned and operated industry, which depended totally on the success of irrigation and sugar beet cultivation in the surrounding countryside. In its first year, the Billings Sugar Company contracted with local farmers for seven thousand acres of sugar beets. By August 1906, the sugar beet refinery was finished and ready to process the year's crop. Its initial capacity could convert 55,000 tons of beets into 161,000 bags of sugar.[21]

Until the oil boom of the mid-twentieth century, the Billings Sugar Company dominated the regional economy as had no other business in the history of Yellowstone County. During seasonal peaks, its number of employees jumped to over seven hundred. It contracted with area farmers for tens of thousands of acres of sugar beets, a steady enough potential income to attract thousands of new residents to the valley. By 1913, for example, area farmers harvested 23,000 acres of beets. Due to its rail connections, its irrigated fields, and solid entrpreneurial base, Billings was better poised than any other Yellowstone community to take advantage of the early twentieth-century homestead boom. With P.W. Moss as chairman, it even hosted the influential Dry Farming Congress of 1909, where boosters, agricultural experts, and railroad executives convinced many that irrigation wasn't even necessary in the Yellowstone as long as you practiced the latest in dry tilling techniques. In fact, successful dry farming experiments in Dawson County—which dated to 1905—seemed to prove the experts right.[22]

The lure of irrigated lands, the promise of dry farming, and less restrictive federal homesteading laws in 1909 and 1912 contributed to the great rush of homesteaders that swept through the Yellowstone valley from 1909 to 1914. Billings had already grown a staggering 211 percent since the last census in 1900, as urban development kept pace with the growth in the valley's rural populatiion. Ten thousand homestead entries were made at the Billings office alone over the five-year period, a land rush that created several large rural communities in Yellowstone County. By 1910, 352 families had filed on almost 21,000 acres at Huntley. Downriver around the new town of Sidney stood the Lower Yellowstone Project, another Reclamation Act program that opened with seven thousand acres of irrigated land in 1909. It greatly boosted the population of the lower valley, and by 1914 Richland County, with Sidney as the county seat, had been carved out of Dawson County. By 1920, the area that had served as Dawson County twenty years earlier had been split into six counties, with 25,000 residents. The lower Yellowstone then experienced a second boom in 1924 when the Holly Sugar Company opened a state of the art refinery at Sidney.[23]

At the height of this homesteading prosperity, in May 1918, Moss, O'Donnell, and their partners sold the Billings Sugar Company to the Great Western Sugar Company, a large corporation that controlled much of the western sugar market. Great Western further expanded production and continued to modernize the factory throughout the next two decades, adding a $500,000 pulp-drying plant, for example, in 1933. Soon after taking control, Great Western began to import immigrant families from Mexico to work the beet fields, a labor strategy the company followed throughout the western reclamation projects. These workers lived in a company-established *colonia* near the sugar beet factory. Mexican officials believed that the sugar company wielded considerable economic and political influence in Billings. "In reality," reported the Mexican counsul at Salt Lake City in 1932, "the sugar company runs the city and county government."[24]

With major refineries at Billings and Sidney and later at Hardin, cultivating and processing sugar beets served as a key to the economic expansion of the Yellowstone valley during the early twentieth century. Another key lay with the exploitation of the Yellowstone's coal reserves, energetically pursued by the Northern Pacific Railroad at Red Lodge, southwest of Billings on the north side of the Beartooth Mountains, and by the Chicago, Milwaukee, St. Paul, and Pacific Railroad at Klein, in the Bull Mountains north of Billings. In 1924, the Northern Pacific would begin strip-mining the vast surface coal reserves at Colstrip, south of Forsyth. Civic capitalists like banker Preston B. Moss of Billings also had fueled the region's expansion by their enthusiasm and investments. In the 1910s, Moss developed grandiose plans for a new Yellowstone industrial center named Mossmain near the Laurel railroad yards. Moss hired noted landscape architect Walter Burley Griffin to draw a city plan, a gracious example of "City Beautiful" planning on the Northern Plains. But a lack of investors, the homesteading bust, and indifference of the railroads eventually spelled doom for Mossmain. Nothing exists there today. The region's railroad network remained perhaps the most important single influence on the Yellowstone's economic development, not only because of its transportation links but also because rail titans like James J. Hill had been among the most important supporters of the homesteading boom. In 1907, the arrival of the Milwaukee Road, which ran along the Yellowstone from Terry to Miles City, further improved the region's rail connections. The company's decision to locate a division point at Miles City boomed its population like no other event since. By 1920, according to geographer John Borchert, Billings had clearly emerged from the pack of Yellowstone towns to be among the ranks of the mid-sized urban centers of the West. Its excellent transportation links made it one of the most important trade centers in the Northern Plains.[25]

But the good times of the early 1900s soon gave way to the bad times of the 1920s and 1930s. The amazing population growth of Billings recorded in the 1910 and 1920 censuses slipped to a meager 8 percent in the 1930 census. And the slow growth recorded in Billings was even more pronounced in other Yellowstone towns. Miles City, for instance, reached 9,000 residents in 1917, but in the late 1930s the WPA's *Montana* guidebook listed only 7,175 residents. The population loss was far worse in the rural communities, many of whom literally disappeared during the homesteading bust that began in about 1919. For many rural residents of the Yellowstone valley the Great Depression came early, and stayed.[26]

New forces would shape the Yellowstone economy after 1940, especially the oil industry. As early as 1914, Charles E. Perkins told Louis W. Hill, then president of the Great Northern Railway, of possible oil deposits in the Big Horn Basin. In 1915, geologists discovered oil at Elk Basin, just south of the Montana state line in Wyoming. In less than a year, 26 wells were in production, and by 1917 the field produced an average of 4,200 barrels of oil a day. In 1922, natural gas was discovered at the Elk Basin field and the Ohio Oil Company promptly built a $2 million pipeline to bring the gas to Billings. The next important strike came at Cat Creek in present-day Petroleum County, north of Billings in central Montana.[27]

None of the early strikes were in Yellowstone County, but seven major oil and gas fields were located within one day's travel from Billings. Where better to establish oil company offices and production facilities than Billings, with its excellent rail links to the rest of the country? As F.H.V. Collins, who operated a small oil company out of Billings, remarked to Louis Hill in 1921, "Just now there are a great many people coming into Montana who seem to be possessed to spend their money." In the spring of 1929, the Yale Oil Company built a two-thousand-barrel capacity refinery along the Yellowstone River at Billings, and as the oil flowed in rapidly from strikes in Stillwater, Big Horn, and Carbon counties, the company later that year

expanded production to six thousand barrels a day. Billings, because of its
geographical location and rail access, became the oil processing center of
eastern Montana.[28]

Due to a lack of investment capital and weak demand, oil and natural
gas exploration proceeded slowly during the Great Depression. In 1936, a
five-well field was established at the Mosser Dome in Yellowstone County.
After the war, however, oil companies aggressively explored the countryside
in search of major deposits, which led to a ten-year frenzy of oil discovery
and development that turned Billings into a modern city, a small counterpart
to the great Texas and Oklahoma boom towns of those same years.[29]

The census takers of 1940 found a much different settlement landscape
between Livingston and Miles City than that chronicled in 1880. Well over
100,000 people now lived in a place clearly marked by three generations of
railroads, irrigation, federal land policy, extravagant and exagerated
agricultural promotion, and the exploitation of mineral resources. Towns and
villages abounded, although many were not more than tiny grain-gathering
points; there was even an emerging urban center in Billings. The Yellowstone
had lost its frontier in exchange for joining the mainstream of American
economy and society.

creating a new community in the north: mexican americans of the yellowstone valley

laurie mercier

The Yellowstone River wets the richest agricultural lands in eastern Montana. Since the early twentieth century, irrigation projects and the nation's sweet tooth have made sugar beets the most profitable and enduring crop grown. Unlike agricultural products such as grain and livestock, which demand little more than the labors of a single family, sugar beets have required an army of temporary workers to thin, cultivate, and harvest the persnickety roots. Mexican Americans have provided much of this essential labor, yet their contributions have gone unheralded. This essay traces the history of the Mexican Americans who came to the Yellowstone as seasonal workers and created a vital ethnic community, which has persisted despite years of economic hardship, discrimination, and cultural and social change.

Long before Montana became a state, Hispanic explorers, trappers, miners, and *vaqueros* were among the first non-Natives to visit the region. After the United States annexed the northern half of Mexico in 1848, many Latin Americans continued to migrate to the north, but it was not until the 1920s that Mexico's dramatically increasing population and an expanding western U.S. economy combined to persuade millions of residents to seek work across the border. By 1930, more than one thousand Mexicans and Mexican Americans had come to the Yellowstone valley.

Federally financed reclamation projects transformed the arid West in the early 1900s, including the Yellowstone valley, where Billings capitalist I.D. O'Donnell and other local businessmen invested in growing sugar beets, an expensive and labor-intensive crop. They incorporated the Billings Sugar Company in 1905 and built one of the largest sugar beet factories in the world the following year. A dozen years later, during the height of wartime agricultural demand, the Great Western Sugar Company bought the factory and encouraged area farmers to plant beets instead of wheat. Beets became a profitable investment up and down the Yellowstone, and Great Western became Montana's (and the nation's) largest sugar producer. Holly Sugar Company also built factories in the region at Sidney in 1925 and at Hardin in 1937.

Profitable sugar beet production required a reliable supply of low-cost labor, which the Montana labor market could not supply. Sugar companies began to recruit from areas where labor was more abundant and from groups of people who had been denied access to other kinds of employment. In 1921, Great Western's Labor Bureau in Denver recruited 385 beet laborers from "southern points" in Texas, California, Colorado, and Mexico for Montana farms. Two years later, the company reported that most of the 500 workers they imported were "of the Mexican type," the beginning of a seven-decade reliance by the beet industry on cheap labor from the American Southwest and Mexico. Government and industry worked together to maintain this employment niche for Latinos. Even when many Americans clamored for immigration restrictions in 1924, for example, growers lobbied for unrestricted movement of Mexican labor and Congress exempted Mexicans from new immigration quotas.

The Great Western Company cultivated its dependence on two ethnic groups to tend valley beets. In 1924, it brought to Montana 3,604 Mexicans and 1,231 German Russians to harvest a record 31,000 acres that year. But the company had different long-range plans for each ethnic group. Great Western loaned money to its German Russian growers, hoping to attract their peasant relatives, who could provide temporary labor for thinning and harvests and eventually become tenants and even landowners. This Company encouragement, along with kinship ties, community acceptance, and ready adjustment to Montana's climate, probably explains why 77 percent of the German workforce remained in the Billings district that winter, a sharp contrast to just 25 percent of the Mexicans. Company actions reflected American racial assumptions that European immigrants made more capable landowners than Mexicans, who many insisted were more suited to agricultural labor than farming.

The racist underpinnings of American culture, together with restrictive legislation and hiring practices, hindered Latino economic mobility, and the low wages made agricultural labor a family endeavor. Families migrated and worked together as a unit and sold their collective labor to farmers. This pattern of family migration and family wage-work shaped the character of the Yellowstone's Latino community and helped maintain fairly equal male to female ratios. It also stimulated the growth of a settled community. Sugar companies, which sought to maintain a stable workforce, promoted family settlement by providing transportation, labor contracts, and housing for families.

The Great Western and Holly Sugar companies created *colonias* near their factories to encourage Mexican workers to "winter over" in Montana. In 1924, the Great Western Company invested improvements in the Billings *colonia*, which housed forty-two families. Mexican laborers built ten new adobe apartments, cindered streets, extended the water line, constructed a drainage ditch, and leveled and planted grass on the compound grounds. Severo "Sal" Briceno came with his family to Billings in 1928, and he recalled that the forty-odd adobe homes of the *colonia* each had one bedroom, a woodstove, and an outhouse. Briceno's family of nine spread into two of the small homes. Residents were responsible for upkeep, and the factory donated tar to patch pervasive leaks in the flat roofs. An outdoor water faucet served every five houses, and when temperatures dipped, Briceno remembered, "we'd have to go out there and make fires around it to unfreeze it."

As in other industrial labor arrangements, settled families fostered a stable workforce, and the *colonias* helped families remain and survive on their meager wages. *Colonia* residents could raise chickens, pigs and gardens to supplement their diets. The company also created a winter jobs program on the factory grounds, believing that in the spring "there would not be a big debt hanging over [farmworkers'] heads, making them more willing to work in the territory rather than to leave . . . in order to get away from their debts." The *colonia* provided a clinic and school for migrant children and unified the Latino community. Esther Rivera recalled that her father, Fred Duran, "used to talk about the *colonia* all the time. Everybody knew everybody. The people really hung together."

As the *colonia* provided the immigrants with a sense of community, it also isolated them from other residents, while their growing numbers also arroused prejudice. The Great Western Company campaigned against the baseless fears directed at its Latino labor pool. During the 1920s, the Company's annual reports emphasized that Mexican laborers had "solved the farm labor problem," that many were U.S. citizens, and that they were skilled workers. These reports concealed the racial tensions that predominated in white Billings.

During the first half of the century, people who spoke Spanish and/or were perceived as "Mexicans" faced great discrimination in Billings. Sal Briceno recalled that Latino children could not participate in the annual Kiwanis Easter egg hunt in South Park: "They had men on horses riding around that South Park kicking us out. There were a lot of kids that wanted candy, but they'd kick us out." Latinos were banned from the public swimming pool, segregated in theaters, and not allowed in restaurants. Signs above some Billings business doors read, "No Mexicans or dogs allowed." Mexican Americans knew racism's unwritten rules and the boundaries of acceptable behavior. Robert Federico's four aunts and mother had vivid stories of "where they could go and could not go." If they could endure stares and taunts, for example, they could venture into the local skating rink. But most places, such as bowling alleys, were off limits. Sal Briceno noted "they [whites] would have kicked me in the head with a bowling ball" if he had ventured there. Barred from most stores, Mexican Americans were dependent on their farm employers to do their shopping.

Farmworker families usually came as part of a crew or group of families recruited. Robert Rivera's family was part of a trainload of Californians who were recruited and promised "opportunities" in Montana during the 1920s. Once in Billings, farmworker families often stayed at the St. Louis Hotel on Montana Avenue across from the depot, while they waited for the Great Western Sugar Company to match them with farmers and take them to the farms. The Riveras and other families, who wintered over for beet planting in the spring, stayed in the *colonia* until the Company transported them once again to Custer, Hysham, Belfry, Joliet, and other places where farmers needed labor. The company also arranged credit at the local grocery until workers were paid and brought farmworkers back to the *colonia* at the end of the beet season. But with limited earnings, families faced many a grim winter. Rivera recalled that his family and most others took their beet earnings to Sawyer's on 29th and invested in bulk groceries:

> That's where most of the people traded, and if they had 3-400 dollars
> to spend on groceries for the winter, they would buy in big lots, flour
> by the 100-pound, coffee by the 25-pounds, lard by the 50-pounds,
> and as much groceries as they could afford they'd take in provisions
> for the winter. Of course when that was gone, that was it.

Some migrant workers developed lasting relationships with farmers and sought to renew their associations each spring, while some other families remained with farmers throughout the year and helped in feeding cattle and mending fences during the winter while they waited for the beet season to begin. As Robert Rivera noted, these arrangements helped sustain farmworker families and also initiate permanent resident status:

> If they wanted you to stay, a lot of times they would offer you the
> place to stay for the winter if you wanted to. Then the men would
> work for them . . . which was better than moving back to the colony,
> because once you moved back there was nothing to carry you
> through the winter.

Mutual friendships often developed between female farmworkers and owners because of shared concerns about children's welfare, or for female companionship on isolated farms. Farm women frequently helped with childcare, dispensed advice, and supplied eggs and other farm products to supplement their workers' earnings. Maria Cantu usually took her children with her to the fields, but when it was too cold, she often left them with the female farmowner, who she fondly remembered: "This lady was just like my mother. She was nice and so sweet." Esther Rivera recalled that a farm woman taught her mother "how to cook American food, she learned how to do everything there. She let her have her own garden spot to raise a garden, so we were very fortunate there."

The beet cultivation cycle changed little over time. In mid-April, farmers began planting; workers hoed and thinned from late May to mid-July. Until farmers began mechanizing and applying herbicides in the 1950s, many migrant families remained over the summer to weed and through the fall to harvest and top the beets. The stoop labor and distinctive tools--a short-handled hoe for thinning and curved knife for topping--also remained the same. "You worked backbreaking long hours," Esther Rivera recalled: "everything was done by hand." It was arduous work, as Sal Briceno remembered, but there were few choices. "The work was hard, [but] you had to do it, you had no alternative." As Esther Rivera remembered it, "both parents really working day and night to keep eight of us children going. You didn't think anything of the work because it was your way of life."

Latino parents often had to care for young children while they worked and children assisted as soon as they were old enough. Dora Cantu recalled that her father always carried an extra hoe in the car; when one of his children reached eight or nine years, he enticed them to "help mom out" so they could go home early. Her mother distracted her children from the drudgery by telling folktales, which often featured children and animals and emphasized cooperation and sharing, crucial themes in the lives of families dependent on the contributions of all their members to survive.

Economic realities also forced many married women to do fieldwork, sometimes on the days when they went into labor and gave birth. As in most American families, the "double day" prevailed for female farmworkers, extending work into the evening: "Father would sit down, mother would cook, she would wash clothes . . . . no one questioned it, all the women were in the kitchen, all the men ate."

When possible, families sacrificed women's critical field labor to manage the household, to cook, and to care for young children and boarders. Ruth Contreraz remembered her mother "practically cooking all day long" to feed her family and ten male boarders who helped her husband work beets. Women often raised gardens and chickens for food, and created clothing and household goods from available materials, such as feed sacks. Many women found time also to make functional products more attractive. "I don't know how she found the time," Esther Rivera recalled of her mother's determination to create beauty in her family's home:

> She made the quilts, she made our clothes, she made homemade cheese, she made everything from scratch, plus she always had time to embroider every pillowcase . . . and had everything fancy. I guess that was their way of expressing . . . having something beautiful for themselves.

The 1930s depression halted recruitment of Latino laborers and the government even deported many to Mexico, including U.S. citizens. In the Yellowstone, opposition to the employment of migrant workers compelled the Great Western Company to hire local workers before hiring outsiders. The company also agreed to employ "solos" from outside the district to discourage families from "remaining and becoming a charge on relief." This reversal of the company's earlier promotion of family settlement resulted in a reduction of wintering employees from 221 in 1935 to 173 in 1937.

Spurred by labor demonstrations across the nation during the 1930s, many farmworkers protested poor wages and working conditions. Yellowstone farmworkers, like other agricultural workers, faced numerous obstacles in labor organizing. Often without supportive communities and dependent on individual growers for jobs, farmworkers were vulnerable to companies and growers, who could retaliate by ejecting rebellious families from housing, refusing to pay back wages and transportation, and importing replacement workers. Nonetheless, from 1934 through 1937, Beet Workers Union strikes and threats of strikes periodically interrupted thinning and harvests, reminding sugar producers of the workers' importance. In 1937, the Yellowstone Growers' Association and beet laborer representatives settled on a piecerate of $21.50 per acre, or $9.50 for thinning, $2.25 for hoeing, $1.35 for weeding, and $.70 per ton for topping.

Second World War production demands and labor shortages generated new calls for Mexican and Mexican American agricultural workers, but new opportunities in defense work on the West Coast, armed services recruitment, and other industry jobs beckoned the nation's Latinos. In the

Yellowstone Valley, the percent of acres thinned by local Mexican American farmworkers steadily declined during the war years, from 44 percent in 1941 to just 9 percent in 1946. Sugar companies and growers frantically pursued workers from the Southwest, and increasingly from Indian reservations, local high schools, German prisoner-of-war camps, and the Japanese American internment camp at Heart Mountain. With fewer resident Latino families interested in farm labor, Great Western resumed its recruitment efforts, soliciting by mail and by personal visits to Mexican American prospects in California and Texas.

Wartime demand was so great that Western growers and agricultural industries in 1943 pressured Congress to create the "bracero" program, Public Law 78, which allowed farmers to employ Mexican nationals to harvest crops. Under the program's agreement with the Mexican government, employers paid transportation and living expenses, provided individual contracts, and promised not to undercut existing wages. From 1943 through 1946, the Great Western's Billings district relied on Mexicans to thin up to 30 percent of its beet fields, and top up to half its crop in the fall when labor was even more difficult to procure.

After the war, farmers accelerated their demand for beet labor and the sugar companies assisted. Santos Carranza began his 33-year career as a labor recruiter for Holly Sugar Company in Sidney during the war. As field office supervisor, Carranza traveled to Texas each spring and distributed cards announcing Montana employment needs, located workers, and advanced money for the trip north where he linked families with lower Yellowstone farmers. After 1963, when Congress terminated the bracero program, companies continued recruiting workers to assure contract farmers of sufficient labor.

Many migrant workers in the Yellowstone Valley sought permanent jobs and better livelihoods, and some actually purchased farms. Anastacio and Brigida Carranza brought their family to the lower Yellowstone from Colorado in 1925 to work beets, and ten years later they managed to buy their first beet farm near Sidney. Maria Cantu and her husband came to the Yellowstone Valley in 1951 with a south Texas contractor's team that worked Great Western's fields in Colorado and Montana. Maria wanted to keep her children from a life on the road, so despite the hardships she insisted that her family find a way to stay in Montana. The Cantus felt lucky to find year-round employment with the same Worden-area farmer for eleven years. They saved and purchased a small farm in 1962, while they continued to thin and harvest beets for area farmers. To supplement the family income, Mr. Cantu periodically worked during harvest loading beets on trains at Pompey's Pillar, Worden, Huntley, Shepherd, and Park City, and also during the winter at the sugar factory.

Farmworker families generally left agricultural work for better paying, steady jobs as soon as they could. As Robert Rivera explained: "The Spanish people would work the fields and work their hearts out trying to make a living, but there was nothing in return, nothing like social security or retirement." But it was not easy to find alternative work. Workers occasionally were hired to "work the beet cars" in the wintertime, unloading beets for factory processing. "It was hard work, cold, working through the night," as Robert Rivera reported, "but then it meant that you had a better chance to go through the winter." Still, widespread discrimination limited opportunities for Mexican Americans, as Sal Briceno remembered, because "they'd get white people for the better jobs." Race was a factor in finding any kind of employment: "There was a lot of discrimination in those days. If you were of Mexican descent, you couldn't do nothing."

Mexican American women often took wage jobs to ensure their family's survival. Esther Rivera believed that Mexican American men—not unlike the men in the larger society—felt "embarrassment if your wife worked" outside the home, before social mores began to change in the 1970s. But economic realities often defy popular ideals. Robert Rivera remembered that his mother had to work "out of the home," cleaning hotels to provide for the family. And Mexican American women also faced discrimination. Esther Rivera recalled that there was considerable employment discrimination during the 1940s and 1950s. She had taken a business course in high school in 1949, for example, but when she sought advertised jobs the doors were often closed. "I applied for jobs all over town and I couldn't get anything, so I had to take a dishwashing job."

Landing a job with the Northern Pacific Railroad or a Billings factory was often Mexican Americans' first real break. "Most of your Spanish people here in Billings," Robert Rivera believed:

since they started working for the railroads, that's what really made a
better life for them, because they got steady work, and they got pretty
good pay, and the majority bought their little house and moved up,
educated their children, and they got retirement from the railroad.

Ralph "Chino" Armendariz was one such success story. He came with his
father to the Yellowstone in 1936 to work beets, and in 1939 he was hired as
a section laborer for the Northern Pacific where he worked until he
retired in 1964.

The Second World War was a watershed period for the nation's
Latinos. When veterans returned to their communities and sought
non-agricultural jobs, many insisted on equal treatment. Robert Rivera and
his five brothers, who served in the military while many of the area's
EuroAmerican residents received deferments to work in agriculture, felt
strongly: "I've fought for this country, and my brothers have fought for this
country, and we feel like we belong here just like anybody else." Rivera
became an ironworker and welder, while his brothers became carpenters. Sal
Briceno chose to drive a Yellow Cab after his release from service, and Ynes
Contreraz worked at Pierce Packing Company from 1948 to 1982, receiving
several promotions and feeling no discrimination. Contreraz believed that
discriminatory practices at local businesses discouraged Mexican applicants,
but "when younger people saw Pierce hiring Mexicans, they knew they had
an alternative to working beets."

Mexican American young people eagerly sought non-agricultural
work. Robert Rivera remembered as a teenager longing for a different life:

> "I would just say to myself when I was in those fields, 'I hope to God
> I never have to do this again, and as soon as I'm able I'm gonna get
> out of here and never do this again.' And I did."

Esther Rivera claimed that "all" Mexican American youth were determined
not to live farmworker lives:

> "We just got out the minute we were fifteen or sixteen and didn't have
> to work in those fields, then you'd do anything else. When I turned
> sixteen I applied for my first job at Billings Laundry."

Yellowstone Valley Latinos believed that education was key to attaining
the American Dream. Beginning in the 1940s, when many farmworkers
acquired their own transportation to "come and go everyday to the beet

fields," many families moved to Billings and other towns to secure year-round schooling for their children. "My dad felt that we were not getting enough education," Ruth Contreraz remembered. "They would always tell us, you kids have to continue going to school no matter what, so you guys can end up with better jobs." Esther Peralez's parents also remained in the Yellowstone Valley so their children could attend school. She recalled a phrase repeated by "everybody's Mexican parent," including her father: "to study so you learn so you're not ignorant like we are." Her father emphasized the importance of education as "what you have to do to get out of [beet work] because I don't have a choice." Parents repeatedly sacrificed and labored long hours, hoping that their children would prosper. Dora Cantu remembered that her mother had been educated in Mexico and had hoped to be a teacher:

> That was her dream to be a schoolteacher, and she was denied this. She always dreamed that one of us would be a schoolteacher. From the time that we were little, 'you've got to learn, you've got to learn to read, you've got to learn to do this. You don't always want to be out here working beets. . . . Go to school and learn. If you don't, this is the kind of life that you'll have.'

Two realities hindered children's education: family economic needs and discrimination. Spring thinning and fall harvesting schedules, for example, placed difficult demands on schoolchildren. Dora Cantu and her sister missed school on alternate days to watch younger siblings while their parents worked beets, and they also adapted work schedules to accommodate school:

> We would get up at four o'clock in the morning, we would work until an hour before the bus would come and pick us up. We would be out until six or seven. We would go down to the house, or we would take our clothes to the field with us, change from our work clothes into our school clothes, run and catch the bus, go to school, come home, and then work again until sundown. This was from early spring when they started thinning beets until we got out of school in June. Then in the fall, when they were topping beets, we would get up again in the frost, and we would go out and pile beets. . . . We'd stack them in the evenings, we'd do at least two or three of those rows, enough so Mom and Dad would have enough beets the next day to top. . . . Sometimes it'd be dark when we went home.

Cantu remembered that Mexican American children, whose parents had a small farm or worked for the railroad, were able to attend school regularly; those who did farm labor often had to drop out. Her parents emphasized the importance of school, so despite the interference of farm labor, she struggled to learn, even though she missed out on important instruction—such as how to calculate percentages—that hindered her.

Although parents supported them, many children encountered prejudice from students and teachers. Ruth Contreraz remembered her experience at Garfield School, where the city's Mexican American students attended classes:

> We were a minority, and we never felt that the teachers defended us in any way. When we got accused of anything, they would go as far as saying well don't even come back to school if you don't want to. They just did not accept us.

Fights erupted when Mexican American youth refused to ignore racial slurs, such as "dirty Mexican, or "greaser" and "bean eater." Ruth Contreraz's mother told her to disregard taunts, but she beat up kids who called her names and then feared her mother would discover that she had been fighting: "We were already thinking why don't Mom and Dad stand up a little bit for our rights. . . . [When] the ones with authority, the teacher and principal, don't defend you in any way or form, even I started hating school." Contreraz "begged" her father to let her drop out of school and go to work. He agreed to allow her to stay out for one year; she never returned. Nonetheless, she insisted that her own children remain in school so they would not "have to work as maids or go through what I had to."

Education provided many Mexican American parents and youth with a greater awareness of their stake in American society. Ruth Contreraz believed that "with education you start recognizing your rights. . . . The younger parents felt they were going to get their kids educated and they can live where they want, we don't have to hold back anymore." But racism and their children's poor performance in the schools convinced many parents that mere access to education was insufficient. Contreraz noted, "That's when I feel that our parents started thinking, no, this is not right, our kids are not getting the education they need. First it was because we lived in farms, and a

lot of the kids had to work, so they would always kind of lag behind."
Mexican American parents began joining PTAs and voicing
their complaints.

During the 1960s, many of the Yellowstone's Mexican American
youth, influenced by the Chicano civil rights movements, worked to change
social attitudes and increase educational and employment opportunities.
Robert Federico, who was inspired by VISTA anti-poverty volunteers while
still a student at Rocky Mountain College, began organizing the Latino
community to combat discrimination, improve housing, increase voter
registration, and promote affirmative action hiring. Esther Peralez, who had
worked in Oregon and observed many militant Chicano students demanding
equal rights, returned to Billings in the early 1970s and joined Federico and
others in mobilizing the Mexican American community to pressure the city
to hire a Chicano school counselor and help more young people enter
college. At that time, she recalled, there were many Latino social activities—
dances and picnics, and cultural events, such as *Cinco de Mayo* celebrations—
but few organized attempts to challenge the Billings city government and
implement reforms.

Latino youth often clashed with their elders over their reform goals
and their militancy. Older residents wanted to preserve cultural traditions
and promote community events, while younger people wanted social change.
"We just did not click," Robert Federico recalled, between "those who
wanted to go slower, and those who wanted to move faster." Another activist
explained that many preferred working quietly behind the scenes to effect
change: "When we have wanted something, we have never done it like they
do in the big cities. Hispanics there will raise their fists and are very
demanding." Jim Gonzalez, a Mexican American leader and respected
Billings city council member from 1977 to 1985, represented the "old school"
belief in working slowly through the system. Federico represented the
younger generation's more aggressive assertion of reformist demands and
opposition to discrimination. Esther Peralez saw the differences as
generational. She remembered her mother's complaints about one young
activist: "'What is his problem? Things are good now. He should have been
here when we were younger, because they wouldn't allow Mexicans in school,
they would beat them up. Things are good now.'" But, as Peralez recalled, her
generation's thinking was different: "We were saying, 'no that's not good

enough. We shouldn't be thankful. . . . There should be rights that everybody has.'" Still, Peralez and other youth felt "cultural frustration," because "in our culture you respect your elders, and I was taught that way," even though she disagreed with their tactics.

By the mid-1970s, second- and third-generation Mexican Americans had established several political and cultural associations to improve the welfare of Billings area Latinos. Since the 1920s, Yellowstone Latinos had organized dances to raise money to help families burdened by hospital debts or victimized by the legal system. Beginning in the 1960s, community members chartered more formal groups. The Latino Club sponsored cultural events and sought to preserve Mexican history and culture. *Concilio Mexicano*, composed of educated, middle-class Hispanics, advocated jobs and education programs for their community. The Mexican American Community Organization (MACO) tried to coordinate Mexican American organizations' activities and responses to crises that affected the larger Latino community. Nevertheless, young and old frequently united on major issues, such as successfully lobbying the city to take action on an incidence of police brutality and persuading the *Billings Gazette* to curb stereotypical coverage of area Latinos.

The Billings South Side neighborhood had long been the heart of the Yellowstone's Latino community. As the traditional home for many of Billings' immigrants and industrial workers, the South Side accepted the new migrants while other neighborhoods did not. They continuted to established permanent homes there, Robert Rivera believed, because they felt "more like being around your own people." Some Mexican Americans who joined the middle class later chose to move away from their South Side roots to other parts of the city. Esther Peralez moved to the Heights, she explained, as part of living out "the American Dream." As someone who grew up in poverty, she wanted "a piece of that pie," "to have a brand new home made from scratch," instead of the older housing available on the South Side. Esther Rivera's family also moved from the South Side to the Heights, but they missed their former neighborhood and ties they had kept since moving to the valley:

> The minute I could drive I was back down there. We attended all the
> social functions, we went to the same church. . . . [my dad] used to
> like to go to the Mexican dances. If there wasn't a dance, he'd make

one, he'd sponsor one. We never lost contact with our [South Side] friends. . . . My parents were very social. They met all these people at the colonia, and they never forgot them.

The South Side's major landmark, Our Lady of Guadalupe Catholic Church, has played an important role in solidifying the Yellowstone's Latino community during the last forty years. Most farmworkers were devout Catholics, but poor transportation and Sunday work demands often prevented them from attending church. Nonetheless, families made special efforts to give their children proper religious instruction. Dora Cantu remembered her father working in fields close to the Ballantine Catholic Church when his children needed to take first communion lessons. Yellowstone Latino families attended a variety of Catholic churches but they desired a setting that nourished their culture. To that end, Sal Briceno helped build the Little Flower Catholic Church on the South Side in the early 1930s. But a increasing white membership in the new church, Briceno felt, soon began "pushing the Mexicans away." Esther Rivera also "never felt like Little Flower was our special church. We always felt like we might be a little in the way." In the early 1950s, as Ruth Contreraz recalled, residents began planning a special ethnic church:

> I think what helped a lot was when a lot of the older Mexican people started talking about how we should have our own church and how we should-better our own community. . . . I think all the different circles at St. Ann's and other churches started talking about developing this and that. They would hold meetings and then everyone had their say on what they felt, what they wanted. . . . That's how it started changing.

After its construction in 1952, Our Lady of Guadalupe Church attracted Latinos from Ballantine, Huntley, and other Yellowstone communities as well the sizable South Side Mexican American community. "We could attend mass anywhere," Esther Rivera explained, "but there we congregated because we need to keep continuity in the community. You're at home." Other residents, such as Liz Castro, agreed that the church attracted people with ethnic, kin, and neighborhood ties: "Everybody knows everybody, it's just a neat place to be." Esther Peralez tried attending other churches in her Heights neighborhood, but she was drawn back to Guadalupe: "It was like old home week. You fit right in, you know people, it's just a comfortable place. . . . So many places, I'm always the only minority, and I think when is this ever going to end . . . you can always pick up subtle discrimination. . . . But going to Guadalupe I always feel comfortable."

In addition to providing for the spiritual needs of the Latino community, the church strengthened ethnic identity Esther Rivera explained: "Before that we were unified, but yet kind of distant, each to his own. But when the church started out, that's when all the people started thinking more or less alike." The church enhanced ethnic pride by providing a gathering place for people to organize cultural events such as *Cinco de Mayo* and September 16 (*die Ciseis*) celebrations. "They used to celebrate . . . in little surrounding towns like Huntley, Worden, Ballentine," Ruth Contreraz remembered, "but here in Billings, nothing . . . because there was no place to get started with it." Since Our Lady of Guadalupe's inauguration in 1952, Contreraz believed that Yellowstone Hispanics "have really come a long ways. . . . Now our culture is being recognized, we have identity, and it's being shared by many other nationalities besides us." The annual December 12 celebration commemorates the day when the Virgen de Guadalupe appeared before Mexico's Juan Diego. After a special mass, the congregation sings to the Virgin and girls present flowers to the church altar. Celebrants then adjourn to the church hall for more singing, refreshments, and pinatas. Before Christmas, parishioners celebrate another Mexican tradition in the processions of *Las Posadas*. Participants reenact Mary and Joseph's search for lodging and share Christmas greetings, refreshments, and songs.

Before building Our Lady of Guadalupe, Yellowstone Latinos made both formal and informal attempts to preserve their Mexican heritage. In 1929, Mexican Americans in Billings formed *La Honorifica Mexicana* to celebrate fiestas on the important Mexican holidays, *Cinco de Mayo*, which commemorates the courageous Mexican defeat of an invading French army in 1862, and the 16th of September, Mexican Independence Day. At these fiestas, Robert Rivera recalled, older men in the community would often discuss the history of Mexico. "They were the ones that really carried the tradition and remembered the customs and everything from the old country. They tried to teach that to the younger people." Adapting traditions to Montana's harvest schedule and unpredictable weather, Billings organizers in recent years have combined the May and September commemorations in one August celebration.

Cultural activities, especially with music, took place on a more informal basis among extended families and groups of friends. Sal Briceno recalled: "Everybody used to get together to sing. I don't think there was a Mexican man who didn't know how to sing and play guitar, and dance the *juarabe tapatilla*." People frequently organized dances, which engaged many area Mexican American bands, such as Little Joe and the Alegres, Harold Garza and the Rebeldes, and Andy Martinez and the Bandoleros. Other residents have periodically sought to preserve and perpetuate Latino culture. Ruth Contreraz, for example, organized a group of young women to learn and perform traditional Mexican dances.

Food arts are often the most persistent cultural activity among American ethnic groups. Yellowstone Latinos introduced the region to a cuisine that has become a standard feature in many restaurants and households. Many women still proudly prepare dishes and employ methods learned from their Mexican mothers and grandmothers. Maria Cantu described how she makes tortillas from scratch, shunning packaged varieties:

> I don't even use corn meal or masaharina. I plant my own corn, I cook my own corn, I grind my own corn, and I use my own corn I let the corn dry, and shell it and put it away in a barrel. Anytime I need it . . . I have a machine to grind it. I cook the corn with lime, and it takes the shell off, and I have to watch it until it turns completely white.

For holidays and special occasions, women sometimes joined other female kin and friends to prepare traditional foods. Sal Briceno remembered his mother often joined with three or four families to buy and roast a pig and then make tamales with pork or turkey and spices for holidays. "All the women would get together" to scrape the meat off the skull, and make *chicharrones* and flour torti11as.

A few women combined their culinary expertise with business acumen and opened restaurants in Billings. Hermina Torres, who came to the Yellowstone Valley with her husband in 1940 as migrant farmworkers, opened Torres Cafe in 1963; her daughter, Josie Torres Quarnberg took over the operation in 1977. Liz Castro and her family operated the El Paso Cafe during the 1980s. The restaurant opened on S. 29th Street, then moved to Montana Avenue to serve "the South Side people."

The Yellowstone's Latino community often faced difficult choices. Sometimes they had to sacrifice cultural identity to obtain greater respect and economic prosperity. Many second-and third-generation Mexican Americans hoped acculturation would engender tolerance. Sal Briceno, for example, recalled that his family was "more Americanized" and therefore "treated better" by the dominant society. But assimilation into the larger community often made economic class rather than "race" the significant factor in distinguishing Latinos. Esther Rivera thought that the larger community became more tolerant when "we became middle class," and that farmworker families became middle class because they "wanted something different for our children," and struggled to attain a more prosperous lifestyle. But the poorer migrant farmworkers were still viewed as the "other" in racial terms, by many non-Latinos in the Yellowstone. Gaining acceptance and opportunity in the larger community has sometimes been won at the expense of cultural cohesion, which has troubled many Yellowstone Latinos who regret the loss of the Spanish language and other aspects of cultural identity. In this respect, the Yellowstone's Latino community has faced greater obstacles than Spanish-language communities in the Southwest and the nation's larger cities, where the density of ethnic populations has provided a measure of ethnic security and diminished the demand to assimilate. Sal Briceno noted that his children lost interest in traditional Mexican music because "there are so many things that they can do now." Traditional culture was no longer central to their lives. "Their culture doesn't mean anything, they're Americans. They consider themselves just as 'white' as anybody else." Intermarriage between the children of EuroAmericans and Mexican Americans, however, has provided a mixed blessing. "So what's happening is our race is getting very diluted." Esther Rivera noted, "You're losing your language, you're losing a lot there. I see it with every generation it's more and more. . . . They don't have memories, they're losing a lot of their culture."

The decline of Spanish as a second language for third- and fourth-generation Mexican Americans alarms many, while some parents remember problems they faced learning English and insist on speaking English to their children. Ruth Contreraz remembered her frustrations as a child trying to learn English in school: "I thought, darn it, when I get married and have children I'm going to talk to them in English. I love my culture, and I'll teach my kids anything to do with my Mexican culture, but English is the important language now. I didn't want my kids to go through that." Families were forced to choose between their language and their children's success. When her older brother failed the first grade because he could not speak English, Esther Peralez's parents resolved to do "whatever we have to do to get you through school," and they "spoke in Spanish, and we spoke in English." Peralez noted that Billings is unusual because so many Chicanos understand Spanish but cannot speak it: "It's sad, but that was the tradeoff in order to survive in these schools." The Yellowstone Mexican American experience illustrates the dilemma of cultural pluralism in the United States, where "either/or" demands to assimilate to avoid discrimination and enjoy equal opportunity often impede the formation of dynamic ethnic cultures that can play an equal and beneficial role in society.

Economic and educational success eluded many resident Latinos. Augie Lopez, who became Billings' first counselor for Latino students in 1973, found an "astronomical" dropout rate because of a hostile school environment and poverty. But increased bilingual instruction dramatically improved conditions and the retention rate. In 1980, concerned Latinos initiated the Eastern Montana College Hispanic Student Scholarship Fund Board to increase Chicano college enrollment. Esther Peralez, a counselor at Eastern Montana College, lamented that still too few Chicano youth were graduating to college, but since the 1980s area educators have begun to link educational progress to positive ethnic identity and have worked to improve cultural sensitivity. In 1990, Latinos comprised almost half of Garfield School's students and their parents actively participated in school activities to foster cultural awareness. At an annual teacher-appreciation day, for example, they present homemade tortillas and Mexican paper flowers.

Mexican American school populations increased in Billings because economic changes made the Latino community more urban rather than rural. Beginning in the 1950s, when agriculture became more mechanized and some discriminatory barriers in urban employment lifted, the state's Latinos began moving to Billings. In 1950, 31 percent of Montana's Mexican-born population resided in urban areas; by 1960, 60 percent lived in cities. By 1980, only 2 percent of Yellowstone County's Hispanic residents were involved in agriculture. This shift in employment patterns reflected general trends in the Northwest region, as Latino immigrants "settled out" and moved to larger towns and cities for jobs and the comforts of an established ethnic community.

The mechanization of the beet industry substantially reduced immigration to Montana. Sal Briceno noted, "We have very few people that come in here now to work beets. Most of it's mechanical now." Merle Riggs, former labor recruiter and agricultural manager for the Billings plant, explained that herbicides greatly reduced the need for hand labor, and allowed "workers that came up here to perform more acres per day." A severe wild oats infestation in the 1950s and 1960s prompted Billings area growers to apply chemicals before other states because they did not have alternative crops to grow. By 1976, an era had ended, when the Great Western Company stopped furnishing transportation for migrant workers, transferring the burden to individual growers and migrant laborers.

In addition to the declining need for farmworkers, declining blue-collar work opportunities discouraged Latinos from settling in the valley. Railroad and packing plant jobs have disappeared, and as Robert Rivera noted, "There was just hundreds of Mexicans working at those [packing] plants, so when those plants shut down, by golly that put a hardship on this town." Esther Rivera agreed that a vital economy was essential to a flourishing Latino community: "A lot of your people have gone and settled elsewhere, and stayed away. Like my aunt and uncle left. We lost a lot of people in our Hispanic community because of the economy, because they will go where the work is."

Despite farm mechanization, beet growers still depend on hand labor. Every spring, about six thousand migrant farm workers—mostly Mexican Americans from the Rio Grande Valley of Texas—come to the Yellowstone to work, following a migrant route that takes them on to Oregon to top and bag onions, to Washington to pick apples, and to Minnesota to harvest beans before returning to Texas in late fall. Successful farmworker organizing during the 1960s and 1970s, however, provided families with benefits not available to their predecessors. In 1972, for example, the Montana Migrant Council was established to provide labor, health, housing, and educational assistance to migrant families. Many Yellowstone Mexican Americans, who retained ties with families from Texas, often worked with federal migrant programs. Parishioners at Our Lady of Guadalupe Church have also extended aid to farmworker families, helping newcomers find housing, farm employment, and food. Ruth Contreraz noted that, "The Mexicans that were settled already in the Hispanic community were helping the migrants that

were coming in . . . because a lot of them knew what it was like to
be a fieldworker."

Despite their importance to the area economy, many Montanans refuse
to acknowledge that migrant farmworkers have permanent connections to
this place, even though Mexican American families return year-after-year to
the same area farms. The term "migrant" is a misleading title for many
Latino families who loyally return to the Valley each spring. Just as many
Montana "snowbirds" annually escape winter's icy grip for the warmer
Southwest, many Texans routinely join the "migrant stream" to thin beets
each cool Montana spring. Some, such as Juan Montes, have been migrant
farmworkers for several decades and have not realized their dream for more
settled employment or a "piece of land" to farm. Others, who consider Texas
their home, continue to work beets during the summer to supplement family
incomes. Mario Iracheta, a Texas construction worker, has come to the
Yellowstone to work beets since 1952 and has children who were born here.

The persistence of the Yellowstone's Latino community is distinct in
the Northwest and Rocky Mountain West. The Hispanic population in
Colorado and Idaho, for example, has grown dramatically in the last few
decades, but Montana's has remained relatively stable and constant with the
rest of the state's population. Scant economic opportunities draw fewer
working immigrants to the Big Sky Country, and declining infusions of
Spanish-speaking immigrants challenge the established second- and
third-generation Billings community to retain links with their ethnic
heritage. Yet Latinos young and old in the Yellowstone continue to find
meaning in family reunions, traditional celebrations, religious observances,
and other social, cultural, and political activities. Like their predecessors,
third- and fourth-generation Mexican Americans continue to honor their
history and reshape their cultural identity.

The Latinos who moved north to the Yellowstone Valley have left a
vital legacy to the area's heritage. The region's agricultural prosperity,
according to one former migrant, depended on the essential labor of Latino
farmworkers: "If it hadn't been for the Mexicans, the farmers wouldn't have
succeeded." Besides their crucial economic role, Mexican Americans have
contributed an enduring ethnic community and enriched the
Yellowstone's culture.

notes

Oral History Excerpts

These oral histories are part of "Real West: Portraits of Farming and Ranching Families in the Yellowstone Region," a public history project that examines the realities of life on the agricultural "frontier" in the Yellowstone Valley from 1880 to 1940. The collection includes thirty-two taperecorded audio interviews and two video productions. The collection is located in the archives of the Western Heritage Center in Billings, Montana. Public access to the collection is permitted with permission of the archives staff (406)256-6809, Ext. 23. All interviews were conducted by Rom Bushnell, staff historian for the project and the Western Heritage Center.

Charles Banderob interview, February 2, 16, 1993, Ballantine, Montana

Santos Carranza interview, August 28, 1993, Sidney, Montana

Joe Medicine Crow interview, March 25, 1993, Billings, Montana

Charles L. "Lester" Gilbert interview, November 3, 1993, Livingston, Montana

William J. "Red" Killen interview, July 23, 1993, Miles City, Montana

Whit Longley interview, July 22, 1993, Forsyth, Montana

August Sobotka interview, August 26, 1993, Glendive, Montana

Lillian Stephenson interview, April 6, 1993, Wilsall, Montana

Birdie Streets interview, April 20, 1993, Pryor Creek, Montana

"In the Yellowstone: River, Myth, and Environment"

1. Joe Medicine Crow, "The Crow Migration Story," *Archaeology in Montana* 20 (September-December 1979): 63-72; Arapooish, Chief of the Crows, "My Country," as told to Robert Campbell, in William Kittredge and Annick Smith, eds., *The Last Best Place: A Montana Anthology* (Helena: Montana Historical Society Press, 1988), 189; Northern Pacific Railroad, *The Climate, Soil and Resources of the Yellowstone Valley* (St. Paul: Pioneer Press, 1882), 14.

2. Alan R.H. Baker, "Introduction: On Ideology and Landscape," in Baker, and Gideon Biger, eds., *Ideology and Landscape in Historical Perspective* (Cambridge: Cambridge University Press, 1992), 1-4; Denis Cosgrove, *Social Formation and Symbolic Landscape* (London: Cambridge University Press, 1984), 4; Yi-fu Tuan, *Space and Place: The Perspective of Experience* (Minneapolis: University of Minnesota Press, 1977), 149-150.

3. Tuan, *Space and Place*, 154.

4. E.H. Schulz, "Examination and Survey of Yellowstone River," *Report of the Secretary of War* (December 30, 1910), 62nd Cong., 1st sess., 1911, H. Doc 83 (Serial 6116), 3-5.

5. William R. Keefer, *The Geologic Story of Yellowstone National Park*, Washington: U.S. Geological Survey Bulletin 1437, (Washington: GPO, 1972), Chapter 1; Walter Harvey Weed, *The Glaciation of the Yellowstone Valley North of the Park*, Bulletin of the U.S. Geological Survey, No. 104 (1893), 53rd Cong., 2nd sess., 1893, H. Misc. Doc 179 (Serial 3254), 13-15.

6. *The Journals of Lewis and Clark Expedition*, Gary Moulton, ed., III:234, 241-242, VIII:228, 231-232, 278, 388; Abraham Nasatir, ed., *Before Lewis and Clark: Documents Illustrating the History of the Missouri, 1785-1804* (St. Louis: St. Louis Historical

Documents Foundation, 1952) 2:381; W. Raymond Wood and Thomas D. Thiessen, *Early Fur Trade on the Northern Plains: Canadian Traders among the Mandan and Hidatsa Indians, 1738-1813* (Norman: University of Oklahoma Press, 1985), 130-200.

7. C. Adrian Heidenreich, "The Native Americans' Yellowstone," *Montana the Magazine of Western History* 35 (Autumn 1985): 2-17.

8. Richard White, "Animals and Enterprise," in Clyde Milner II, et al., eds., *The Oxford History of the American West* (NY Oxford University Press, 1993), 245-247.

9. Aubrey L. Haines, *The Yellowstone Story* Vol. I (Boulder: Colorado Universities Press, 1977), 68-73; Richard A. Bartlett, *Nature's Yellowstone* (Albuquerque: University of New Mexico Press, 1974), 126-128; Aubrey L. Haines, ed., *The Valley of the Upper Yellowstone: An Exploration of the Headwaters of the Yellowstone River in the Year 1869* (Norman: University of Oklahoma Press, 1965).

10. W.F. Raynolds, *Report of the Exploration of the Yellowstone River in 1859-60*, Sen. Ex. Doc. 77, 40th Cong., 1st sess., July 1, 1867 (Washington: GPO, 1868), 53-54.

11. Raynolds, *Report*, 10, 15, 40-41, 45. Perhaps part of the explanation for Raynold's focus on aridity is explained by the fact that his immediately previous army posting had been in damp and humid Florida.

12. William E. Lass, "Steamboats on the Yellowstone, " *Montana the Magazine of Western History* 35 (Autumn 1985):27-31; Carroll Van West, *Capitalism on the Frontier: Billings and the Yellowstone Valley in the Nineteenth Century* (Lincoln: University of Nebraska Press, 1993), 61-63.

13. Thompson P. McElreath, *The Yellowstone Valley: What it is, Where it is and How to get to it. A Hand-Book for Tourists and Settlers* (St. Paul: Pioneer Press, 1880), 75-77; *An Illustrated History of the Yellowstone Valley* (Spokane: Western Historical Publishing Company, [1907]), 277; Billings Gazette, *Illustrated Historical Edition* (1899), 1.

14. *Billings Gazette: Illustrated Edition* (July 1894), 24.

15. West, *Capitalism on the Frontier*, 136-137, 194-196; Michael P. Malone, Richard Roeder, and William L. Lang, *Montana: A History of Two Centuries* (Seattle: University of Washington Press, 191), 233-234; Edward Holtzheimer, "Down the Yellowstone Forty Years Ago," *Pacific Monthly* (January 1908):77; "Work Begun on Big Ditch," *Anaconda Standard*, December 18, 1903.

16. Donald Worster, *Rivers of Empire* (NY: Oxford University Press, 1988),191-256; Malone, et al., *Montana*, 234-236.

17. Donald Worster, *An Unsettled Country: Changing Landscapes in the American West* (Albuquerque: University of New Mexico Press, 1994), 44-46; Frank R. Grant, "To Husband the Land: Robert Sutherlin and the Irrigation-Dry Farming Controversy," in Rex C. Myers and Harry W. Fritz, *Montana and the West: Essays in Honor of K. Ross Toole* (Boulder: Pruett Publishing Company, 1984), 87-104; Major E.H. Schulz, U.S. Army Corps of Engineers, *Examination and Survey of the Yellowstone River*, 62nd Cong., 1st sess., 1911, H. Doc 83 (Serial 6116), 2-19. The Intake dam was authorized in 1905 and completed in 1910.

18. M.M. Galbraith, et al., *Report on Proposed Project for Flood Control and Irrigation in the Yellowstone River Valley* (Livingston: Yellowstone Irrigation Association, 1921), 8-12.

19. William L. Lang, "Saving the Yellowstone," *Montana the Magazine of Western History* 35 (Autumn 1985):88-89; *Livingston Enterprise*, June 17, 1920.

20. "General Conditions," (1934), Memorandum SL 16 (1935), Lower Yellowstone Irrigation Project, Nick W. Monte to W.H. Jones, May 31, 1935, Federal Resettlement Administration Collection, MC 206, Montana Historical Society Archives, Helena; Commissioners of Wyoming and Montana, *Division of Waters of the Yellowstone River* 74th Cong., 1st sess., 1935, S. Doc. 20 (Serial 9909), 2; Richard A. Bartlett, *Yellowstone: A Wilderness Besieged* (Tucson: University of Arizona Press, 1985), 354-358.

21. Clyde L. Seavy, *Division of the Waters of the Yellowstone River*, 76th Cong., 1st sess, 1939, S. Doc. 362 (Serial 10293), 3; *Agreement for Division of the Waters of the Yellowstone River*, 76th Cong., 3rd sess., 1940, H. Doc. 2336 (Serial 110442), 2-5; *Yellowstone River Compact*, 78th Cong., 2nd sess., 1944, S. Doc. 674 (Serial 10841), 2-6; *Compact Relating to the Waters of the Yellowstone River*, 82nd Cong., 1st sess., 1951, S. Doc. 883 (Serial 11490), 2-5; Andrew C. Dana, "An Evaluation of the Yellowstone River Compact: A Solution to Interstate Water Conflict," (M.A. thesis, University of Washington, 1984), 12-15. The compact divided the waters in the following allotments: Clark's Fork of the Yellowstone—Wyoming 60%, Montana 40%; Big Horn—Wyoming 80%, Montana 20%; Tongue—Wyoming 40%, Montana 60%; Powder—Wyoming 42%, Montana 58%. North Dakota was assured of an apportioned percentage of water diverted at Intake.

22. National Park Service, *Reconnaissance Report of Recreation and Development on Allenspur Reservoir, Yellowstone Division, Montana* (National Park Service, 1962).

23. Montana Department of Natural Resources, *How the River Runs: A Study of Potential Changes in the Yellowstone River Basin* (Helena: DNRC, 1981), 17-20.

24. Ibid., 5-8; See also K. Ross Toole, *Rape of the Great Plains* (Boston: Atlantic, Little, Brown, 1976), and Richard L. Reese, ed., *Coal Forum* (Missoula: Montana Committee for the Humanities, 1974).

25. Constance Boris and John V. Krutilla, *Water Rights and Energy Development in the Yellowstone River Basin: An Integrated Analysis* (Baltimore: Johns Hopkins University Press, 1980), 129-130. The authors estimated the water use intensity of coal-fired steam plants as 60 times greater than just mining the coal.

26. Department of Natural Resources, *How the River Runs*, 8; Boris and Krutilla, *Water Rights and Energy*, 255-262.

27. Department of Natural Resources, *Inventory of Water Resources in the Yellowstone River Basin*, (Helena: Department of Natural Resources, 1976), 134-136; William J. Grenney, "Utilizing Scientific Information in Environmental Quality Planning," *American Water Resources Association* (Minneapolis, September 1979), 105-110.

28. Dean Krakel II, *Downriver: A Yellowstone Journey* (San Francisco: Sierra Club Books, 1987), xvii.

29. Bill Richards, "The Untamed Yellowstone," *National Geographic* (August 1981):256-278; Lang, "Saving the Yellowstone," 89; "Yellowstone's Future is Tourism," *Independent Record*, January 8, 1992; "Subdivision Survey," draft 1994, Greater Yellowstone Coalition, Bozeman, Montana.

"A Cheyenne History"

"A Cheyenne History" is based on an interview with Bill Tall Bull which was conducted by George Horse Capture at Dull Knife Memorial College in Lame Deer, Montana on April 26, 1993. Transcripts of the interview are available in the Western Heritage Center archives.

"An Undeniable Presence: Indians and Whites in the Yellowstone Valley, 1880-1940"

Abbreviations:

ARCIA   Annual Report, Commisioner of Indian Affairs

RCA, FRC   Records of Crow Agency, Federal Records Center

LR, OIA   Letters Received, Office of Indian Affairs

1. See George C. Frison, *Prehistoric Hunters of the High Plains*, 2nd edition (San Diego: Academic Press, 1991), 39-40; Wilfred M. Husted, *Bighorn Canyon Archeology*, Reprints in Anthropology, Volume 43 (Lincoln, NE: J. & L. Reprint, 1991; originally published as Volume 12, Smithsonian Institution River Basin Surveys: Publications in Salvage Archeology, 1969), 1-67. Much of this narrative is based on Frederick E. Hoxie, *Parading Through History: The Making of the Crow Nation in America, 1805-1935* (NY: Cambridge University Press, 1995).

2. ARCIA, 1872, 834.

3. Col. Hatch to Adjutant General, February 16, 1882, OIA LR, 1882- 4892, RG 75, NA; Henry Armstrong to Commissioner of Indian Affairs, June 23, 1882, OIA LR, 1882-12066, RG 75, NA; Lt. Hugh L. Scott to Post Adjutant, Fort Meade, D.T., May 29, 1883, enclosed with John Tweedale, Chief Clerk to the Secretary of War to Secretary of the Interior, July 13, 1883, OIA LR, 1883-12905, RG 75, NA. Accusations against the Crows can be found in Armstrong to Commissioner of Indian Affairs, April 7, 1882, OIA LR, 1882-7643, RG 75, NA; Secretary of Interior to Commissioner of Indian Affairs, January 14, 1882, OIA LR, 1882-1042, RG 75, NA; Governor Hoyt to Secretary of the Interior, June 12, 1882, OIA LR, 1882-10918, RG 75, NA; Secretary of War to Secretary of Interior, June 12, 1882, OIA LR, 1882-11009, RG 75, NA; Secretary of War to Secretary of the Interior, June 9, 1883, OIA LR, 1883-10648, RG 75, NA; and William Hale, Governor of Wyoming, to Commissioner of Indian Affairs, November 9, 1883, LR OIA, 1883-20708, RG 75, NA.

4. Proceedings of Council of July 19, 1881, Item 3, Box 9, RCA, FRC, Seattle.

5. The visit of Young Man Afraid of His Horses is in Henry Armstrong to Commissioner of Indian Affairs, November 13, 1883, Item 2, Box 1, RCA-FRC, Seattle; Two Moons and Roman Nose are discussed in Armstrong to Capt. E.P. Ewers, June 26, 1884, Item 3, Box 10, RCA- FRC, Seattle; Visits of Gros Ventres are discussed in Armstrong to "Gifford," October 7, 1884, Item 3, Box 10, RCA-FRC, Seattle and Henry Williamson to A.J. Gifford, February 22, 1886, RCA-FRC, Item 4, Box 12; on Crow peacemaking, see H.Heth to CIA, September 1, 1886, LR-OIA, 1886-24401, RG 75, NA. My interpretation of the Sioux visit to the Crows is confirmed by a description of a friendly visit of Omahas to a Yankton camp in Ella Deloria's *Waterlily* (Lincoln: University of Nebraska Press, 1988), 107. I am grateful to Raymond DeMallie for pointing out this reference.

6. "Proceedings of a Council of the Crow Indians held at Crow Agency, Montana Territory, Friday, April 23, 1887." Enclosed with Williamson to Commissioner of Indian Affairs, May 6, 1887, Special Case 133, LR-OIA, 1887-12645, RG 75, NA.

7. Report of remarks by Plenty Coos (sic), made to the agent on February 20, 1890, 7432-1890, LR-OIA, RG75, NA.

8. S. Exec. Doc. 43, 51st Cong., 2nd sess. (Serial 2818), 11.

9. See "Proceedings of Council With Crow Indians," filed as 1899- 45587, LR-OIA, RG75, NA, October 31, 1898, p.8. The high price insisted on by the tribe held up the final sale of the lands described in the 1898 agreement for nearly six years.

10. Hearings Before the Committee on Indians Affairs, U.S. Senate in S.2087 and S.2963, S.Doc. 445, 60th Cong., 1st sess., 776.

11. S. Doc. 445, 60th Cong., 1st sess. (Serial 5260), 771, 772, 773, 774.

12. On the hiring of Kappler and Merillat, see Reynolds to Commissioner, June 28, 1909, Item 2, Box 8, RCA, FRC, Seattle. The petition, dated June 17, 1909, is in Container B122, Indian Affairs File-Kappler and Merillat, Part I, Robert Lafollette Papers, Library of Congress (hereafter Lafollette Mss). In making this request, tribal leaders may have acted on the suggestion of Helen Grey, a journalist who had spent time on the reservation and who was then living in Washington. She had urged them to hire a lawyer, or they may have contemplated filing a suit before the United States Court of Claims. Grey opposed the Kappler and Merillat firm. See Grey to Herbert Welsh, March 1, 1909, IRA Mss, Reel 21; Council minutes of February 18, 1909, enclosed in Reynolds to Commissioner, September 30, 1909, Item 2, Box 8, RCA, FRC, Seattle. According to the council minutes, Plenty Coups said, "every now and then I hear of a tribe of Indians getting a big chunk of money on some old land matter. They have taken a big lot of country from the Crows that we were never paid for...." In June of 1909, Two Leggings wrote to the Secretary of the Interior that, "We want a lawyer in whom we have confidence to look after our interests."(Two Leggings to Secretary of the Interior, June 11, 1909, IRA Mss, Reel 21). A final possibility is that Kappler and Merillat were suggested by Robert Lafollette, then a member of the Indian Affairs committee. See Brosius to Sniffen, December 30, 1909, IRA Mss, Reel 21. On the Business Committee, see: Reynolds to Commissioner of Indian Affairs, November 15, 1909, Item 2, Box 8, RCA, FRC, Seattle. For Holcomb's report, see "E.P. Holcomb, Supervisor, Submits the Results ...", Central Classified Files, Crow Agency, File 150, 18844-10, LR-OIA, RG 75, NA. For comment on 1910 committee, see W.W. Scott to Commissioner of Indian Affairs, January 12, 1911, Item 14, Box 50, Council Proceedings, 1911-1913, RCA, FRC, Seattle.

13. S. Rep. 219, 66 Cong., 1 sess. (Serial 7590), 8-9. For reports of the "success" of the delegates efforts, see Victor Evans to Plenty Coups, September 23, 1919, and Calvin Asbury to "The Crow Indians," October 8, 1919, Plenty Coups Mss.

14. Proceedings of the Council," August 27, 1921, Item 15, Box 77,p.15, RCA, FRC, Seattle.

15. "Proceedings of the Crow Tribal Council, February 12, 1926," 6, Council Proceedings, 1924-1927," Item 15, Box 78, RCA, FRC. Seattle, Washington.

16. Plenty Coups to C.H. Asbury, n.d., Item 15, Box 83, file 131, RCA, FRC, Seattle.

17. Robert H. Lowie, *The Crow Indians* (Lincoln: Univ. of Nebraska Press, 1935), 209.

18. J. Watson to Commissioner of Indian Affairs, January 6, 1896,Item 2 box 4, RCA, FRC, Seattle.

19. ARCIA, 1889, 223; Wyman to Commissioner, March 4, 1892, Item 2, Box 3, RCA, FRC, Seattle.

20. Graves to Commissioner of Indian Affairs, September 1, 1896, 35775-1896; W.B. Hill to Commissioner of Indian Affairs, April 10, 1901, 25893-1901; ditto, February 19, 1903, 11777-1903; October 20, 1904, 81803-1904; and April 21, 1905, 32257-1905; all in Special Case 190, Crow, LR-OIA, RG 75, NA. The 1919 figure is from H. Doc. 387, 66

Cong., 2 sess., 3. See also three histories of the Crow irrigation project, unsigned but apparently prepared by Agent Watson in the late 1890s, in Item 88, Box 244, RCA, FRC, Seattle.

21. Graves to Commissioner of Indian Affairs, August 10, 1895, 45636-1895, Special Case 190, Crow, LR-OIA, RG75, NA.

22. Council Proceedings, August 27, 1892, Special Case 147, Crow, RG 75, NA.

23. "To The Hon. Commissioner of Indian Affairs," May 6, 1912, Item 14, Box 54, Law and Order, 1912-1914, RCA, FRC, Seattle.

"Knowing Our Place: Memory, History, and Story in the Yellowstone Valley"

Many thanks to several people who provided invaluable assistance with this project. David Walter, Reference Librarian at the Montana Historical society in Helena, provided me with a bibliography of local histories from the Yellowstone Valle. Lindsey Miller of the History Department at Montana State University combed through the folklore materials in the Federal Writers Project Collection at Montana State University in Bozeman. And Emily Witcher of the Western Heritage Center in Billings searched through local histories with considerable diligence and intelligence and came up with a body of narratives on which this paper is based.

1. This is true even when these community histories are produced according to guidelines provided by an outside publishing company, such as Curtis Media of Dallas.

2. Big Horn County Historical Society Bicentennial Committee, camp., *Lookin' Back: Big Horn County* (Hardin: Herald Publishers, 1976), 69.

3. Marjorie and Jim Barnard, comps., *North of the Yellowstone, South of the Bulls* (Billings: Northside Historical Publishers, 1978), 12.

4. [Thomas Family story] in author's possession.

5. Elsie P. Johnston, *Laurel's Story, A Montana Heritage* (Billings: Artcraft Printers, 1979), 22.

6. Powder River County Extension Homemakers Council, *Echoing Footsteps: A Powder River County History* (Butte: Ashton Printing Company, 1967), 400-401.

7. Helen Carey Jones, comp., *Custer County Area History: As We Recall* (Dallas, Texas: Curtis Media Corporation, 1990), 320.

8. Local legend collection, Folklore Archives, University of California, Berkeley.

9. Pioneer Society of Sweet Grass County, *Pioneer Memories* (Big Timber: Pioneer Publishers, 1980), Vol. I, 178.

10. Rosebud County Bicentennial History Committee, *They Came and Stayed* (Billings: Western Printing and Lithography, 1977), 43

11. *Pioneer Memories*, I, 26

12. Huntley Project History Committee, *Sod 'N Seed 'N Tumbleweed: A History of the Huntley Project, Yellowstone County, Montana* (Billings: Frontier Press, 1977), 327.

13. Federal Writers Project, Billings Folklore files, Special Collections, Montana State University, Bozeman.

14. Barnard, *North of the Yellowstone*, 47.

15. Miles City Corral of the Range Riders and Range Riders Reps of Custer County,

Fanning the Embers (Billings: Gazette Printing and Lithography, 1971), 482.

16. Mary R. Haughian, *Mildred Memories on the O'Fallon* (Terry, Montana: Privately Published, 1979), 89.

17. Legend Collection, Archive of California and Western Folklore, University of California, Los Angeles.

18. O'Fallon Historical Society, *O'Fallon Flashbacks* (Billings: Western Printing and Lithography, 1975), 430.

19. *They Came and Stayed*, 22.

20. *Pioneer Memories*, I, 241-242.

21. *Echoing Footsteps*, 654.

22. *Echoing Footsteps*, 70.

23. Luella DeVries, comp., *Lest We Forget . . . Shepherd, Montana* (Billings: Frontier Press, 1976), 94.

24. *O'Fallon Flashbacks*, 432.

25. *Echoing Footsteps*, 532.

26 *O'Fallon Flashbacks*, 486.

27. *As We Recall*, 306.

28. *Pioneer Memories*, II, 125.

29. Federal Writers Project, Park County Folklore Files, Special Collections, Montana State University, Bozeman.

30. [tough woman], in author's possession.

31. *Pioneer Memories*, II, 103.

32. *Sod 'N Seed 'N Tumbleweed*, 280.

33. Ruth Carrington and Edna Mackley, eds., *Tales of Treasure County* (Billings: Times Publishers, 1976), 152.

34. Naming Kid Montana, in author's possession.

"Dreamers of Horses"

1. Nannie T. Alderson and Helena Huntington Smith, *A Bride Goes West* (Lincoln and London: University of Nebraska Press, 1969), 211.

2. Ibid., vi

3. Ibid., 212-213.

4. Frank W. Hogeland, "Hogelands in Montana," from *Abraham and Mary Hogeland & Descendants*, ed. R. H. Murray (unpublished MSS, in author's possession), 30.

5. A. B. Guthrie, Jr., *The Big Sky*, (reprint, 1947; NY: Cardinal Edition, 1965), 432.

6. A. B. Guthrie, Jr., *These Thousand Hills* (Boston: Houghton Mifflin, 1956), 3.

7. A.B. Guthrie, Jr., *Arfive* (Boston: Houghton Mifflin, 1970), 28-29.

8. Ibid, 102

9. Abraham Hogeland, unpublished notes [in author's possession].

10. D'Arcy McNickle, *The Surrounded* (reprint, 1936; Albuquerque: University of New Mexico Press, 1988), 22.

11. James Welch, *The Indian Lawyer* (New York and London: W.W. Norton and Company, 1990), 158.

12 Norman Maclean, *A River Runs Through It* (Chicago: University of Chicago Press, 1977), 104.

13. William W. Bevis, *Ten Tough Trips: Montana Literature and the West* (Seattle and London: University of Wasington Press, 1990), 178.

14. Maclean, *A River Runs Through It*, 98.

15. Ruth McLaughlin, "Seasons," *Best American Short Stories*, ed. Joyce Carol Oates (Boston: Houghton Mifflin, 1979), 159.

16. Ripley Schemm, "Songs Were Horses I rode," *Mapping My Father* (Story, Wyoming: Dooryard Press, 1981), 10.

17. Annick Smith, "It's Come to This," *Best American Short Stories*, ed. Robert Stone (Boston: Houghton Mifflin, 1992), 285.

"Imagining Montana: Photographs by Frank J. Haynes, L.A. Huffman, and Evelyn Cameron"

1. Jill Kerr Conway, *The Road from Coorain* (NY: Vintage Books, 1989), 3.

2. Laton Alton Huffman title for a hand-colored photograph in the Western Heritage Center, Billings, Montana [WHC]. The term was widely used for the "empty" range north of the Yellowstone River.

3. For the larger story of how images of the West came to stand for something larger than their immediate subject, see William Truettner, et al., *The West as America* (Washington: The National Museum of American Art and the Smithsonian Institution, 1991), and John Peters-Campbell, "The Big Picture and the Epic American Landscape" (Ph.d. diss., Cornell University, Ithaca, New York, 1989).

4. William Henry Jackson, *Time Exposure: the Autobiography of William Henry Jackson* (reprint, 1940; NY: Cooper Square Publishers, 1970) 196; Beaumont Newhall, *The History of Photography* (NY: Museum of Modern Art, 1982); Roland Barthes, *Camera Lucida: Reflections on Photography* (NY: Hill & Wang, 1981), 4; Susan Sontag, *On Photography* (NY: Dell Publishing, 1973), 56.

5. Oliver Wendell Holmes, *The Professor at the Breakfast-Table* (Boston: Houghton Mifflin, 1859), 191.

6. Carroll Van West, *Images of Billings: A Photographic History* (Billings: Western Heritage Press, 1990), 7, 9, 20; Donna M. Lucey, *Photographing Montana, 1894-1928: the Life and Work of Evelyn Cameron* (NY: Alfred A. Knopf, 1991), 156. Numerous photographic prints in the collections of the Parmly Billings Library in Billings, the Montana Historical Society in Helena, the Montana Historical Collections at Montana State University in Bozeman, and WHC in Billings bear the imprints of these studios and many others.

7. Helena Camera Club, *Catalogue of the First Annual Print Exhibit* (Helena, 1898). The catalogue was donated to the Helena Public Library by the Helena Camera Club. For thorough survey discussions of the practices and techniques of photographers in the West at the time, see Ralph W. Andrews, *Picture Gallery Pioneers: 1850 to 1875* (Seattle: Superior Publishing, 1980); William Crawford, *The Keepers of Light: A History and Working Guide to Early Photographic Processes* (Dobbs Ferry, NY: Morgan and Morgan, 1979); Dorothy Hooler and Thomas Hooler, *Photographing the Frontier* (NY: G.P. Putnam's Sons, 1980). Evelyn Cameron to Miss Grant, 18 March 1926, Box 1, Folder 2,

Cameron Papers, Montana Historical Society, Helena [MHS].

8. See Anne Farrar Hyde, *An American Vision: Far Western landscape and National Culture, 1820-1920* (NY: New York University Press, 1990), 25-26.
9. George Catlin, *Letters and Notes on the Habits and Customs of the North American Indians* (NY: Dover Books,1980); Hyde, *An American Vision*, 205.
10. Nathaniel P. Langford, "The Wonders of the Yellowstone," *Scribner's Monthly* 2 (May 1871); Thurman Wilkins, *Thomas Moran: Artist of the Mountains* (Norman: University of Oklahoma Press, 1965); Peters-Campbell, "The Big Picture," 193.
11. The best sources for information on Haynes's early career are in Freeman Tilden, Following the Frontier with *F.J. Haynes: Pioneer Photographer of the Old West* (NY: Alfred A. Knopf, 1964); Montana Historical Society, *F. Jay Haynes, Photographer* (Helena: Montana Historical Society Press, 1981); Edward W. Nolan, *Northern Pacific Views: The Railroad Photography of F. Jay Haynes, 1876-1905* (Helena: Montana Historical Society Press, 1983); Haynes Collection, MHS; Haynes Papers, Montana Collection, Montana State University Library, Bozeman [MSU].
12. *F. Jay Haynes, Photographer*, 6.
13. Northern Pacific Railway, *Photographs Tell the Truth: Pictures of the Great Northwest* (n.p., n.d.).
14. Norris letter, July 18, 1881, in Haynes Papers, MSU; F. Jay Haynes to Mrs. Haynes, August 3, 1883, in Annals of Wyoming 14 (January 1942).
15. Helena Daily Herald, September 13, 1883, quoted in Nolan, *Northern Pacific Views*, 62.
16. Notebooks and Lily Verna Haynes scrapbooks, Haynes Papers, MSU.
17. For an explanation of "luminism" and its effect on American landscape photography, see John Wilmerding, et al., *American Light: The Luminist Movement, 1850-1875: Paintings, Drawings, Photographs* (Washington: Harper and Row Publishers and the National Gallery of Art, 1980).
18. Northern Pacific Promotional Brochure, quoted in Nolan, *Northern Pacific Views*, 132.
19. See the Huffman Papers, MHS. The only book-length studies of Huffman are Mark H. Brown and W.R. Felton, *Before Barbed Wire: L.A. Huffman, Photographer on Horseback* (NY: Bramhall House, 1956) and *The Frontier Years: L.A. Huffman, Photographer of the Plains* (NY: Bramhall House, 1955). Huffman has also been included in a number of exhibition catalogues, such as C. Adrian and Virginia Heidenreich, *Montana Landscape: One Hundred Years (1830s-1930s)* (Billings: Yellowstone Art Center, 1982), 31.
20. Donna Lucey, Photographing Montana, 183. Janet Williams, the woman on the left in the photograph, is the person responsible for preserving the heritage of Evelyn Cameron. One of Cameron's closest friends, she held nearly the entire collection of Cameron's glass plates until Donna M. Lucey negotiated their publication. What Cameron sold and distributed were fully worked prints for her customers and albums representing her ranch life to her family back in England. We have only the glass plate negatives and only a few of the finished works are now known.
21. Ibid.
22. Janet Williams was a frequent visitor at the Eve Ranch, a close friend of the Camerons, and preserved Cameron's negatives in her cellar in Terry, Montana.
23. Lucey, *Photographing Montana*, 183.

"Good Times, Bad Times: The Economic Transformation of the Yellowstone Valley, 1880-1940"

1. Frederick Billings to Thomas Doane, November 24, 1879, Northern Pacific Railway Papers, Minnesota Historical Society [NP Papers]; Thomas C. Cochran, *Railroad Leaders, 1845-1890: The Business Mind in Action* (Cambridge: Harvard University Press, 1953), 97, 135; John 0pie, *The Law of the Land: Two Hundred Years of American Farmland Policy* (Lincoln: University of Nebraska Press, 1987), 76.

2. Marie MacDonald, *Glendive: History of a Montana Town* (Glendive, Mont.: Gateway Press, 1968), 14-15; Shirley Westlund and Ethel Jordan, "Railroad History in Glendive," *Our Times, Our Lives* (Glendive, Mont.: Dawson County Tree Branches, 1989), 5; *Illustrated History of the Yellowstone Valley* (Spokane: Western Historical Publishing Company, 1907), 373-73.

3. John C. Hudson, "Main Streets of the Yellowstone Valley: Town-Building Along the Northern Pacific in Montana," *Montana* 35 (Autumn 1985):59-65; Park County News, March 3, 1955; *Illustrated History*, 151-152; Carroll Van West, *Capitalism on the Frontier: The Transformation of Billings and the Yellowstone Valley During the 19th Century* (Lincoln: University of Nebraska Press, 1993), 95-96; *Centennial Scrapbook: Livingston, 1882-1982* (Livingston, Montana: Livingston Enterprise, 1982), 25-26.

4. *Livingston Enterprise,* March 17, 1900; *We Will Welcome You to Livingston* (Livingston, Montana: n.p., 1900), n.p.; *Centennial Scrapbook*, 31; *Illustrated History*, 156-158; Carroll Van West, "Livingston: Railroad Town on the Yellowstone," *Montana* 33 (Autumn 1985):84-86.

5. West, *Capitalism on the Frontier*, 210-212.

6. Quote is from Richard C. 0verton, *Burlington Route: A History of the Burlington Lines* (New York: Alfred A. Knopf, 1965), 229-230; *Billings Gazette*, October 6, 1894.

7. Albro Martin, *James J. Hill and the Opening of the Northwest* (New York: Oxford University Press, 1986), 366-392; Julius Grodinsky, *Transcontinental Strategy, 1869-1893: A Study of Businessmen* (Philadelphia: University of Pennsylvania Press, 1962), 391-392; Ralph W. Hidy, et al., *The Great Northern Railway: A History* (Cambridge: Harvard Business School Press, 1988), 72-85.

8. George Stephen to James J. Hill, October 18, and Hill to Stephen, October 20 and 25, 1894, and to Jacob Schiff, January 4, 1895, James J. Hill Papers, James J. Hill Reference Library, St. Paul; Heather Gilbert, *The Life of Lord Mount Stephen, vol. 2, The End of the Road, 1891-1921* (Aberdeen, Scotland: Aberdeen University Press, 1977), 73-75.

9. Edward Adams to Dr. Georg Siemens, March 15; George Stephen to Hill, April 10; Gaspard Farrar to Hill, April 10; Adams to Hill, May 9-10; Hill to Stephen, June 24; and Jacob Schiff to Hill, November 18, 1895, Hill Papers; Martin, *James J. Hill*, 446-450; Gilbert, *Mount Stephen*, 81-83; Overton, *Burlington Route*, 231; Vincent P. Carosso, *The Morgans: Private International Bankers, 1854-1913*, (Cambridge: Harvard University Press, 1987), 384-86.

10. "Memorandum of a Conference held in London on the 2nd of April, 1896," Charles H. Coster and Edward Adams to Hill, July 31, 1896, and Hill to Charles Coster, August 19 and October 29, 1898, and Memorandum of May 31, 1901, Hill Papers; Martin, *James J. Hill*, 462-64; Gilbert, *Mount Stephen*, 94-96; Hidy, *Great Northern*,

90-92; Overton, *Burlington Route*, 250-61; James J. Hill, *Highways of Progress* (New York: Doubleday, 1910), 237.

11. Louis T. Renz, *The History of the Northern Pacific Railroad* (Fairfield, Wash.: Ye Galleon Press, 1980), 205-6; *Livingston Enterprise*, March 17, 1900; *Billings Gazette*, October 30, 1900 and March 19, 1901; Hidy, *Great Northern*, 92-93; Martin, *James J. Hill*, 485-91, 494-511; Hudson, "Main Streets," 65; Elsie Johnston, *Laurel's Story: a Montana Heritage* (Billings: Artcraft Publishing, 1979), 91-94; *Illustrated History*, 302; *10th Annual Report of the Northern Pacific Railway* (New York: Northern Pacific Railway, 1906), 10; *12th Annual Report of the Northern Pacific Railway* (New York: Northern Pacific Railway, 1908), 11-13.

12. John C. Hudson, "Railroads and Urbanization in the Northwestern States," in William L. Lang, ed., *Centennial West: Essays on the Northern Tier States* (Seattle: University of Washington Press, 1991), 190; *Illustrated History*, 290-91; John T. Cumbler, *A Social History of Economic Decline: Business, Politics, and Work in Trenton* (New Brunswick: Rutgers University Press, 1989), 15.

13. Robin W. Winks, *Frederick Billings: A Life* (New York: Oxford University Press, 1991), 256-59; West, *Capitalism on the Frontier*, 119-21, 142-43, 154-55, and 177-78.

14. Ibid., 164-77.

15. Tom Stout, ed., *History of Montana* (Chicago and New York: American Historical Society, 1921), II, 241; *Billings Gazette*, October 6, 1899; Lawrence Small, *A Century of Politics on the Yellowstone* (Billings: Rocky Mountain College, 1982), 94.

16. Stout, *History of Montana*, II, 218; *Illustrated History*, 490; Myrtle E. Cooper, *From Tent Town to City: A Chronological History of Billings, Montana, 1882-1935* (Billings: Privately published, 1981), 38-39.

17. Small, Century of Politics, 56; *Billings Gazette*, July 7, 1894 and October 6, 1899; "Life of a Pioneer as told by I. D. O'Donnell to Ruth Korber, 1933," Western Heritage Center, Billings; O'Donnell Family Scrapbook, Harley O'Donnell Collection, Billings.

18. *Billings Gazette*, October 9 and 12, 1900 and 20th Anniversary Issue, April 1905; S. M. Emery to I. D. O'Donnell, April 4, 1900, I. D. O'Donnell Papers, Harley O'Donnell Collection, Billings.

19. Samuel E. Dove, *A History of the Billings Bench Water Association and its Predecessors 1903-1935* (Billings: Yellowstone County Historical Society, 1984), 6-11; *Irrigation in Montana* (Helena: Montana State Government, 1920), 33-34.

20. William H. Hancock, "Huntley Project Irrigation District," R. H. Scherger, ed., *Sod N Seed N Tumbleweed: A History of the Huntley Project Yellowstone County, Montana* (Ballatine, Mont.: Huntley Project History Committee, 1977), 8-9; Stanley W. Howard, *Green Fields of Montana: A Brief History of Irrigation* (Manhattan, Kansas: Sunflower University Press, 1992), 41-42.

21. Records of Incorporation, 1905, Yellowstone County Courthouse, Billings; Cooper, *From Tent Town to City*, 42.

22. Michael Malone, Richard Roeder, and William L. Lang, *Montana: A History of Two Centuries* (Seattle: University of Washington Press, 1991), 185; Cooper, *From Tent Town to City*, 51; *The Fourth Dry Farming Congress and International Dry Farming Exposition* (Billings: Board of Commerce, 1909); McDonald, *Glendive*, 39; K. Ross Toole, *Twentieth Century Montana: A State of Extremes* (Norman: University of

Oklahoma Press, 1972), 42-45; William G. Robbins, "The Northern Tier States as 'Plundered Provinces,' 1900-1940," Lang, *Centennial West*, 24-26; Howard, *Green Fields*, 63.

23. Hancock, "Huntley Project," 11; *Focus on our Roots: Story of Sidney* (Sidney, Montana: MonDak Historical and Art Association, 1989), 29-31 and 54; Elwood Mead, *Opportunities for Farm Ownership on the Lower Yellowstone Project* (Washington: Bureau of Reclamation, 1927); McDonald, *Glendive*, 38.

24. Note on Sugar Company Dissolution, Harley O'Donnell Collection, Billings; *Billings Gazette*, September 24, 1933; Dennis N. Valdes, "Settlers, Sojourners, and Proletarians: Social Formation in the Great Plains Sugar Beet Industry, 1890-1940," *Great Plains Quarterly* 10 (Spring 1990), 116; Ricardo Romo, "Mexican Americans in the New West," Gerald Nash and Richard W. Etulain, eds., *The Twentieth Century West: Historical Interpretations* (Albuquerque: University of New Mexico Press, 1989), 126-127.

25. John R. Borchert, *America's Northern Heartland* (Minneapolis: University of Minnesota Press, 1987), 75; John V. Goff, et. al., Miles City, *Montana: An Architectural History* (Miles City, Mont.: Star Printing Company, 1988), 47-48 and 53; for more on Hill and homesteader boosterism, see Joseph K. Howard, *Montana: High, Wide, and Handsome* (New Haven: Yale University Press, 1943), 167-177.

26. Federal Writers' Project, *Montana: A State Guide Book* (New York: Hastings House, 1939), 189; Goff, *Miles City*, 53.

27. Charles E. Perkins to Louis W. Hill, June 3, 1914, Oil Papers, Box 1, F.H.V. Collins to Louis W. Hill, April 18, 1921, Box 2, Louis W. Hill Papers, Hill Library, St. Paul; *Billings Gazette*, October 26, 1915 and October 23, 1928; *Wall Street Journal*, November 17, 29, 1920; C.J. Hares, The Elk Basin Oil Field, Bulletin 691-I, United States Geological Survey (Washington, D.C.: GPO, 1918). The original manuscript of this important document is in the C.J. Hares Collection, American Heritage Center, University of Wyoming [Hares Collection].

28. *Billings Gazette*, January 18 and December 22, 1931 and April 21, 1940; Cooper, *Tent Town to City*, 69 and 73

29. *Great Falls Tribune*, September 7, 1946; Malone et al., *Montana*, 256-257; Small, Century of Politics, 81; Oil Scout Reports, Box 17, and see correspondence from 1952-1953, Box 3, Hares Collection.

"Creating a New Community in the North: Mexican Americans of the Yellowstone Valley"

Resources on Montana's and the Yellowstone's Mexican American community are few. This essay relies to a great extent on the reminiscences of Yellowstone Valley Latino residents. In providing a sense of the past and information on elusive topics such as ethnic identity, oral history interviews are a crucial source of information about people in the twentieth century. Interviewers Linda Lee Hickey, Laurie Mercier, Lynda Moss, Nancy Olson, and Wanda Walker intervied Sal Briceno, Maria Cantu, Liz Castro, Ruth Contreraz, Ynes Contreraz, Robert Federico, Dora Cantu Flannigan, Esther Peralez, Don Pippin, Merle Riggs, Esther Rivera, and Robert Rivera as part of the Yellowstone Sugar Beet Oral History Project. the project was funded by the American Association of State and Local History and Western Sugar Company, Tate & Lyle, Ltd. The tape-recorded interviews and transcripts are preserved in the Western Heritage Center's archives. an interview with Santos Carranza of sidney, by Laurie Mercier, is deposited with the Montana Historical Society archives. Also critical to understanding the historical role of Latino beetworkers, or *betabeleros*, were the annual reports of the Billings Sugar Factory and Great Western Sugar Company, produced by factory managers for the years 1917-1950. These records are also deposited with the Western Heritage Center. Clippings and pamphlets in the vertical files of the Billings Public Library, typescripts and reports in the vertical files of the Montana Historical Society library, articles on the Yellowstone Hispanic community in the *Billings Gazette* (appearing more frequently after 1976) also significantly aided research.

The researcher using census records to estimate Latino populations must use caution. Early classifiers branded Mexican people as a "race," ignoring the diversity found within Mexico and the U.S. origins of many Mexican Americans. Official definitions shifted over time, reflected in the confusing Bureau of Census demarcations that range from a racial category, "Mexicans," in 1930, to a more ambiguous language identity, "Hispanic," in 1990. Since 1970, the census came closer to acknowledging ethnic identity by classifying Spanish-language residents, which included second- and third-generation Mexican Americans, in addition to those born in Mexico. Only 7 percent of Montana Hispanic residents in 1970 and 1980 were foreign-born, and close to half were born in Montana, indicating the stability and slow growth of the community. As late as 1990, Montana's 12,000 Hispanics accounted for just 2 percent of the entire state population. Census records, however, notoriously undercount Latinos and often do not include those who identify with the culture but do not consider Spanish their primary language. This particularly applies to Montana and the Yellowstone, where Spanish is more selectively spoken.

The following bibliography indicates the paucity of materials on Latino communities in Montana and the Yellowstone, but these sources will assist those interested in further research. The author extends special thanks to Emily Witcher, Lynda Moss, Wanda Walker, and Dave Walter for their assistance in locating materials, to Esther Rivera for reviewing the manuscript and offering her suggestions, and to the narrators who volunteered their recollections for the WHC oral history project.

Selected Bibliography

Adams, Helen D. "History of the South Park Neighborhood." South Park Neighborhood Task Force and Billings-Yellowstone City-County Planning Board, 1978. Pamphlet file, Billings History, Billings Public Library.

Cardoso, Lawrence A. *Mexican Emigration to the U.S., 1897-1931*. Tucson: University of Arizona Press, 1980.

Devitt, Steve. "We Montanans: The Billings Hispanic Community. *Montana Magazine* (September 1987):6-13.

Gamboa, Erasmo. *Mexican labor & World War II: Braceros in the Pacific Northwest, 1942-1947*. Austin: University of Texas Press, 1990.

Gutierrez, Robert F. "The Montana Migrant Workers." Typescript, 1982. Vertical file, MHS Library.

Hipanic Task Force. "Hispanics in Montana: Report to the 47th Montana Legislative Assembly." Montana Department of Community Affairs, 1980. Vertical file, MHS Library.

Holterman, Jack. "Californios in Far Montana." Unpublished manuscript, 1980. SC 1653, MHS Archives.

Reisler, Mark. *By the Sweat of Their Brow: Mexican Immigrant Labor in the U.S., 1900-1940.* Westport, Connecticut: Greenwood Press, 1976.

Rural Employment Opportunities. Migrant Oral History Project. Interviews by Patricia Nelson. OH 634, MHS Archives.

Slatta, Richard W. "Chicanos in the Pacific Northwest." *Pacific Northwest Quarterly* (October 1979): 155-162.

Spomer. Pete. "History of Sugar Beets." Big Horn County Historical Society Newsletter, n.d. Vertical file, WHC.

Contributing Authors

Mary Clearman Blew earned a Ph.D. in English from University of Missouri-Columbia and is Professor of English at University of Idaho. Blew is the award-winning author of short stories and memoirs set in Montana, including *Runaway* (1990), *All but the Waltz: Essays on a Montana Family* (1991), and *Balsamroot: A Memoir* (1993).

Barbara Allen Bogart holds a Ph.D. in folklore from U.C.L.A. and is a folklorist and historical consultant in Evanston, Wyoming. Bogart is author of numerous articles and books on western folklore and methodology, including *Homesteading the High Desert* (1987) and *Sense of Place: American Regional Cultures* (1990).

Frederick E. Hoxie is Director of the D'Arcy McNickle Center for the History of the American Indian at the Newberry Library in Chicago. Hoxie received a Ph.D. in history from Brandeis and is author or editor of several books on Indian history, including *A Final Promise: The Campaign to Assimilate the Indians, 1880-1920* [1984] and *Parading Through History: The Making of the Crow Nation, 1805-1935* (1995).

William L. Lang is Director of the Center for Columbia River History and Associate Professor of history at Portland State University. Lang earned a Ph.D. in history from University of Delaware and is author or editor of several books in regional history, including *Centennial West: Essays on the Northern Tier States* (1991) and *Montana: A History of Two Centuries* (1991).

Michael P. Malone is President of Montana State University and author of six books on western history, including *The Battle for Butte* (1981), *Montana: A History of Two Centuries* (1991), and a forthcoming biography of James J. Hill.

Laurie Mercier is Program Director at the Center for Columbia River History and Assistant Professor of history at Washington State University-Vancouver. Mercier received a Ph.D. in history from University of Oregon and has researched ethnic and oral history in Montana, Oregon, Washington, and Idaho. Mercier is the author of numerous articles on oral history, public history, and women's history in national and regional journals.

Lynda Bourque Moss is the Director of the Western Heritage Center and Project Director of "Our Place in the West: Places, Pasts, and Images of the Yellowstone Valley from 1880-1940. Moss received an MFA in Arts from Montana State University and has served as an Adjunct Professor of Art at Eastern Montana Colleges. Moss is the recipient of an American Association for State and Local History Award of Merit, and is the author of several articles on museum management.

John Peters-Campbell received a Ph.D. in American Art from Cornell University and is Assistant Professor of Fine Arts History at University of Colorado at Colorado Springs. Peters-Campbell is a specialist on nineteenth-century American painting and is author of *Golden Day, Silver Night: Perceptions of Nature in American Art, 1850-1910* (1983).

William Tallbull is a full-blood elder of the Northern Cheyenne nation and on the faculty of Dull Knife College in Lame Deer, Montana. Tallbull is a Northen Cheyenne tribal historian, the first Native American member of the National Advisory Council on Historic Preservation, a member of the NAGPRA Review Board, and Executive director of the Medicine Wheel Alliance.

Carroll Van West is Projects Coordinator at the Center for Historic Preservation and Assistant Professor of history at Middle Tennessee State University in Murfreesboro, Tennessee. West earned a Ph.D. in history at the College of William and Mary and is author of several books on Montana, including *A Traveler's Companion to Montana History* (1986), *Images of Billings: A Photographic History* (1990), and *Capitalism on the Frontier: the Transformation of Billings and the Yellowstone Valley in the 19th Century* (1993).

index